Wondrous Depth

Wondrous Depth

Preaching the Old Testament

ELLEN F. DAVIS

WESTMINSTER
JOHN KNOX PRESS
LOUISVILLE · KENTUCKY

Unless otherwise indicated, Scripture translations are the author's. Scripture quotations marked "NRSV" are from the New Revised Standard Version of the Bible, copyright © 1989 by the Division of Christian Education of the National Council of the Churches of Christ in the U.S.A., and are used by permission.

Hebrew and Greek fonts: BWHEBB, BWHEBL [Hebrew]; BWGRKL, BWGRKN, and BWGRKI [Greek] Postscript® Type 1 and TrueType™ fonts Copyright © 1994–2002 BibleWorks, LLC. All rights reserved. These Biblical Greek and Hebrew fonts are used with permission and are from BibleWorks, software for Biblical exegesis and research.

Excerpt from "In Memory of W. B. Yeats," copyright 1940 and renewed 1968 by W. H. Auden, from *Collected Poems* by W. H. Auden. Used by permission of Random House Inc. and Faber & Faber Ltd.

Excerpt from "What Is the Crying at Jordan," lyrics copyright by Carol Christopher Drake from *The Hymnal 1982.* Used by permission. All rights reserved.

Illustration on p. 156, St. John of the Cross, *Christ Crucified,* courtesy of Carmelitas Descalzas, La Encarnacion, Avila.

Book design by Drew Stevens
Cover design by Pam Poll Graphic Design
Cover art: In the Beginning by Sandra Bowden. Sandra Bowden (www.sandrabowden.com) is a painter and printmaker living in Chatham, Massachusetts. Her work is a meditation on time incorporating biblical archaeological references, geological formations, segments of language and Hebrew text, inscribed artifacts, and timeworn pages from antique Bibles. Bowden is particularly interested in how the written language allows us to communicate across time and place.

First edition
Published by Westminster John Knox Press
Louisville, Kentucky

This book is printed on acid-free paper that meets the American National Standards Institute Z39.48 standard. ∞

PRINTED IN THE UNITED STATES OF AMERICA
05 06 07 08 09 10 11 12 13 14—10 9 8 7 6 5 4 3 2 1

Library of Congress Cataloging-in-Publication Data is on file at the Library of Congress, Washington, D.C.

ISBN 0-664-22859-3

To Bard, with deep gratitude

Contents

Acknowledgments

This book has been very long in the making. My interest in the connection between biblical exegesis and preaching began in earnest as soon as I started full-time teaching, and so in many respects, the essays here represent thinking I have done with my students over the past seventeen years. But the impetus for writing it down came from the invitation to give the 2003 Beecher Lectures at Yale Divinity School. My first thanks, then, are to Dean Harry Adams and the YDS faculty for issuing the invitation, and to Dean Harry Attridge for hosting the Lectures. Dr. George Sumner, principal of Wycliffe College, University of Toronto, and the Very Reverend Martha Horne, dean and president of Virginia Theological Seminary, also hosted occasions on which I presented a version of an essay in lecture form, and I thank them. A number of people read versions of these essays as I prepared them for delivery, and their comments at various points made me aware of things I had not seen clearly: Stephen Chapman, Stanley Hauerwas, Richard Hays, Margaret Adams Parker, Roger Symon, Barbara Wheeler. In addition to comments, Peter Hawkins and Dwayne Huebner gave me indispensable correction, sometimes over my protests; in every important matter, I eventually came to see that they were right. Daily I am grateful to benefit from Dwayne's wisdom, and I depend upon his patience with what consumes me.

I am grateful to Walter Brueggemann and to Krister Stendahl for long encouraging me, both personally and through their own work, to believe that preaching is a proper concern for a biblical scholar. In complementary fashion, the College of Preachers (at the National Cathedral) has through many years given me the courage of my conviction that premodern biblical exegesis, as evidenced in sermons, can instruct contemporary preachers. The College has been a second teaching home to me, remaining constant while my primary home has periodically changed, and many of the ideas developed here were probably first aired in that gracious place. I thank Erica Wood, Shelagh Casey Brown, James Fenhagen, and Dean McDonald for welcoming me there time and time again. I owe special thanks to my Duke student Brent Scott; his serious study of Lancelot Andrewes renewed and deepened my appreciation of that great preacher's art.

Stephanie Egnotovich of Westminster John Knox Press is always generous, supportive, and astute; what a privilege to have an editor whose comments I can hardly wait to receive. Matthew Olver and Matthew Schlimm assisted ably and conscientiously with preparation of the typescript. It is now hard for me to remember what it was like to write before I worked with Carol Shoun, who has been adviser and friend to me at every stage of planning and editing this book. I am deeply grateful to her, to Dean L. Gregory Jones, and to the superb librarians of Duke Divinity School for creating an environment in which it is a joy to do the work of scholarship.

This book, like the Beecher Lectures themselves, is dedicated to Brevard S. Childs, my teacher, colleague, and friend of more than twenty years. From the outset, he encouraged me to do the kind of biblical scholarship I thought was important for the life of the church. "Those who trust us educate us," as George Eliot wrote. I hope that the work that culminates here has been worthy of the trust he placed in me.

Feast of St. Mary the Virgin
August 15, 2004
Durham, North Carolina

Introduction

Mira profunditas eloquiorum tuorum, quorum ecce ante nos superficies blandiens parvulis, sed mira profunditas, deus meus, mira profunditas! Horror est intendere in eam, horror honoris et tremor amoris.

The wondrous depth of your utterances, whose surface may indeed be flattering to the childish, but the wondrous depth, my God, the wondrous depth! It gives one a shudder to peer into it—a shudder of awe, and a tremor of love.

— *Augustine, Confessions 12.14.17*

The four essays in this volume address what I regard as the gravest scandal in the North American church in our time—namely, the shallow reading of Scripture. Such reading results from the assumption that we already know just what the Bible says; therefore, our reading is a simple rehearsal of what (we think) we know rather than an attempt to probe deeper. The assumption of prior knowledge that is fully adequate to new challenges seems to be widely held by "conservative" and "liberal" Christians alike. Ironically, that common assumption may account for the sterility of the arguments between them. However heated and divisive those arguments may be, they do little to advance the church's understanding of its Scriptures, or even to provoke curiosity[1] about what fresh insight the Bible might offer into the multiple situations that perplex or disturb us, or what new possibilities for our life it might disclose.

In order to gain perspective on our current habits of reading, it is important to recognize that it is a peculiarly modern conceit to assume that we might ever know fully what God has to say to us through the Scriptures. Ancient and medieval interpreters regarded it as impossible ever to plumb that "wondrous depth" and exhaust all its treasure. Therefore, the aim of premodern commentary and preaching was precisely to keep readers and hearers conscious of that *mira profunditas*—and, indeed, hovering over it, praying for illumination by the Spirit that

---

1. I explore the notion that curiosity, understood as both an ethical and an intellectual virtue, is essential to reading Scripture well in my essay "Holy Preaching: Ethical Interpretation and the Exegetical Imagination," in Ellen F. Davis, *Imagination Shaped: Old Testament Preaching in the Anglican Tradition* (Valley Forge, Pa.: Trinity Press International, 1995), 243–67.

hovered over the deep at the creation of the world (cf. Gen. 1:2).[2] If the Bible is indeed the Word of the Living God, revealed and made intelligible to us through the power of the Holy Spirit, then our lack of curiosity bespeaks the failure to be alert to the presence of God in our midst and so refresh ourselves and our tired arguments by returning again and again to the new word that waits to be heard today. Isaiah enables us to hear God's pain at the spiritual laziness or hard-heartedness that prevents us from hearing something unexpected from God:

> I would have been inquired of by those who did not even ask;
> I would have been found by those who did not even seek me.
> I said, "Here I am, here I am!"
> to a people who did not call upon my name.
>
> *(Isa. 65:1)*

The chief point that this book seeks both to argue and to demonstrate is that the activities of biblical interpretation and preaching are essentially related to one another and, moreover, are inextricably connected in the church's life. The modern separation of the two into wholly distinct academic disciplines has obscured that connection. Indeed, it is now widely regarded as axiomatic that one should not do exegesis in the pulpit. Conversely, "homiletical treatments" of Scripture are dismissed by biblical scholars as inherently lacking in substance. This mutual aversion between preachers (or homileticians) and professional exegetes indicates that those who read Scripture for a living, in their several capacities, have largely forgotten that the purpose of exegesis is to edify the church—and that the bulk of Christian biblical interpretation has historically been done in the context of preaching.

My argument is that biblical interpretation and preaching are related precisely as *arts*. The concept of an "art" is richer and more flexible than that of an "academic discipline," although it is essential to remember that the practice of an art involves the exercise of a disciplined imagination as well as certain well-honed skills if the results of our efforts are to be any good. So the central idea I wish to develop here is that biblical interpretation and preaching are the arts most fundamental to the life of the church. I could even say that these two are constitutive of the church, for "faith comes by hearing" (Rom. 10:17). What is distinctively Christian about our proclamation can only be based upon how we read the scriptural tradition and how we live out of what we read.

---

2. The cover art by contemporary artist Sandra Bowden suggests exactly such an understanding of Gen. 1:2.

The claim that biblical interpretation and preaching are intrinsically "artful" does not mean that they are elitist endeavors. It simply means that when practiced seriously, they can never be boring, either to the practitioner of the art or to those who "appreciate" its results. Some years ago, a professor in the art department at a large state university spoke to me about what she hopes to achieve when she teaches drawing and painting to students of more or less ordinary artistic talent. "Very few of my students have any possibility of becoming professional artists. My goal is to teach them how to see, so they never have to be bored again." It sometimes takes a long time to see the full dimensions of a statement that is truly wise. I now realize that is probably the best reason to practice and teach any art, including those of biblical interpretation and preaching: so that we may learn how to see. As Augustine knew from experience, anyone who can see at least a little distance into the depths of Scripture never has to be bored again.

A further implication of my treatment here is that exegesis and preaching are *traditional* arts. We can only interpret the Bible because others have done so before us. Andrew Louth observes that (as he learned from Gadamer)

> in interpreting a piece of writing it is . . . a matter of my listening to what was once written, listening across a historical gulf which is not empty, however, but filled with the tradition that brings this piece of writing to me, and brings me not only that piece of writing but preconceptions and prejudices that enable me to pick up the resonances of the images and arguments used in whatever it is I am seeking to understand.[3]

The tradition that preserves these texts and maintains that they are worth hearing anew in each generation also shapes us as readers. Paradoxically, the text is really *ours* to interpret—and no preacher can speak for or with a text (or even argue with it fairly) without feeling a sense of belonging with it—only insofar as we recognize that we do not read it alone. We are always in the company of other readers, with Christians in multiple generations before us (although, since our tradition is living and changing, we are not likely to be in full agreement with them).[4]

---

3. Andrew Louth, *Discerning the Mystery: An Essay on the Nature of Theology* (Oxford: Clarendon, 1983), 106–7.

4. While it is not my primary focus in these essays, one might (and in a comprehensive treatment of preaching, should) extend the point and say that the community with whom we preachers share a "say" about the text includes also Christians in other places and social circumstances, whose ideological perspective may differ greatly from that of our immediate hearers. Further, "ordinary" Christian preachers are increasingly interested in the fact that we share these same texts with another faith community—and increasingly aware that our "principled" ignorance or contempt of how Jews read them has, ironically, impoverished our own tradition.

Our interpretations and our sermons are then the product of our participation in that multigenerational community of readers. Wendell Berry's comment on the communal nature of writing poetry is apt also to preaching: "Any poem worth the name is the product of a convocation. It exists, literally, by recalling past voices into presence. . . . Poetry can be written only because it has been written. As a new poem is made, *not only with the art but within it*, past voices are convoked—to be changed, little or much, by the addition of another voice."[5]

This book is designed to be a convocation of preaching voices that stretch across centuries. In brief, here I call upon the people who have taught me most about preaching in order to explore issues and problems that arise, sooner or later, for everyone who engages seriously in preaching, and in particular, Old Testament preaching.[6] Can we really believe that these ancient texts, which reflect a world—even, in many respects, a religion—so different from our own, provide reliable guidance for contemporary Christian life? Can preachers draw upon the work of critical biblical and theological study so as to meet the pastoral needs and the urgent questions of their hearers? What I am looking for is a style of reading and preaching the Old Testament that fosters development of an expansive moral vision deeply grounded in the gospel. (By "expansive," I mean open to challenge, to conversation with outsiders, to growth and to change.) I believe that such an interpretive style is most likely to emerge in the context of a theological tradition that maintains a lively awareness of the past and at the same time looks to the future with curiosity and some uncertainty, as well as imagination and hope—all of these informed by faith.

The essays here do not unfold a single argument in linear fashion, nor do they offer a systematic treatment of the topic of Old Testament preaching. Based upon the 2003 Beecher Lectures, delivered at Yale Divinity School, they are closely related (yet independent) explorations of several aspects of biblical exegesis, hermeneutics, and preaching. Chapter 1 advances the view of the Old Testament that I take to be most fruitful for preaching—that the text is an urgent and speaking presence—in contrast to the more common view that we contemporary Christians are separated from the Old Testament by a vast chasm whose dimensions are not just historical but also moral and theological. I turn

5. Wendell Berry, "The Responsibility of the Poet," in *What Are People For?* (New York: North Point, 1990), 89. Emphasis mine.
6. Since this study treats a specifically Christian topic, the avowedly Christian term "Old Testament" seems most natural.

to Dietrich Bonhoeffer as a Christian preacher who felt acutely the immediate presence and pressure of God's Word, especially as heard through the Prophets, and conformed his own words to the Word he heard. Chapter 2 focuses on preaching the Psalms (perhaps the most under-preached book of the Bible) and considers what difference it might make if preachers welcomed the fact that the psalms are poems. I have appended to that chapter a sermon by John Donne, possibly the greatest poet-preacher of the psalms the church has ever produced. Chapter 3 explores the traditional view that any part of Scripture is liable to have more than one meaning. Here I treat the much-debated question of christological preaching of the Old Testament, considering its theological and pastoral potential, as well as the exegetical controls that should inform it. Chapter 4 focuses entirely on the work of one preacher, Lancelot Andrewes (1555–1626), the best single example known to me of the preacher as traditional artist. I chose Andrewes simply because my students and I have learned so much from him. The essay ends with a close reading of his Good Friday sermon of 1604, and I have appended the entire text so that readers may enjoy its full effect.

In calling upon people such as Bonhoeffer, Donne, and Andrewes, I am making personal choices, with no attempt to cover even the high points of the history of interpretation and preaching. Because preaching is an art, the skills it requires are best learned by sympathy, not in abstraction. In these essays, I am watching great artists at work, seeing how they deal with problems and puzzles that the text presents, to Christians at least. I am trying to learn from them basic principles of biblical interpretation and communication of the gospel message as it is found in both Testaments. Although the focus is not on homiletical technique as such, my interest throughout is practical rather than antiquarian: what can ordinary preachers like ourselves learn from these masters of the art? Something of what I have taken from them is evidenced in the several sermons of my own that conclude the book. I offer them not as models but as contemporary examples of how the traditional sensibility developed in the essays has expressed itself in a few specific settings, in response to particular historical circumstances, particular liturgical occasions, and particular texts (in all cases, those appointed by the lectionary). All four sermons are to some degree topical, and I have not attempted to generalize or contemporize their applications. While the details may have changed somewhat, I think the basic elements of our situations have not, nor has the need to read them in light of the whole Christian Bible. That is the essence of the preacher's art.

Abbreviations

ANF	*Ante-Nicene Fathers.* Edited by Alexander Roberts and James Donaldson. 1885–1896. 10 vols. Repr., Grand Rapids, 1978–1981
AT	Author's translation
BB	Bishops' Bible
BCP	*Book of Common Prayer*
CF	Cistercian Fathers. Spencer, Mass., 1970–
CWS	Classics of Western Spirituality. New York, 1978–
FC	Fathers of the Church. Washington, D.C., 1947–
GB	Geneva Bible
ISBE	*International Standard Bible Encyclopedia.* Edited by G. W. Bromiley. 4 vols. Grand Rapids, 1979–1988
KJV	King James Version
LXX	Septuagint
NPNF[2]	*Nicene and Post-Nicene Fathers,* Series 2. Edited by Philip Schaff and Henry Wace. 1890–1900. 14 vols. Repr., Grand Rapids, 1978–1979
NRSV	New Revised Standard Version
OBT	Overtures to Biblical Theology. Philadelphia, 1977–
PG	Patrologia graeca [= Patrologiae cursus completus: Series graeca]. Edited by J.-P. Migne. 162 vols. Paris, 1857–1886
PL	Patrologia latina [= Patrologiae cursus completus: Series latina]. Edited by J.-P. Migne. 217 vols. Paris, 1844–1864

CHAPTER 1

The Art of Astonishing:
Old Testament Preaching

No one would choose a topic so hopelessly broad as "Old Testament preaching" unless she thought there was a broad target to aim at—some difficulty or unease with Old Testament preaching that is widely felt. That some difficulty exists is evidenced by the fact that there is not a lot of Old Testament preaching done these days, at least not in European-American churches. And even when an Old Testament text is treated, often little is attempted with it—little, that is, in terms of serious reckoning with the text itself. In most cases, there is a brief reference to a familiar biblical figure or story as illustrative of the sermon's main point, which is somewhere outside the text and the biblical story.

In my hearing, at least, it is highly unusual for a preacher to linger over a passage and find it compelling of attention, not as an illustration, but as an indispensable source of knowledge about the things of God. How rare it is for a preacher to work deeply with the challenge found in a prophetic passage, or perhaps a narrative, expecting to find *in the text itself* some guidance for meeting that challenge. Rarer still for a Christian preacher to discover in the instructions and prayers of the Old Testament a substantial measure of "the peace of God, which passeth all understanding" (Phil. 4:7)[1]—and then show specifically how these words offer comfort in affliction, companionship in grief, clear direction for our gratitude, and inchoate hope. In sum, it is a rare thing for a

---

1. These words, traditionally part of the priestly blessing at the conclusion of the Anglican communion service, are in that context a summation of the gift of the Holy Spirit that worshipers might pray to receive through hearing the Word proclaimed and preached, as well as participating in the prayers and the sacrament. See BCP, 339.

preacher to show an Old Testament text to be not just useful but truly astonishing, and that absence of astonishment is the puzzling lack with which I wish to work here.

I took my title for this chapter, "The Art of Astonishing," from Jean Leclercq's description of the great twelfth-century preacher and theologian Bernard of Clairvaux. But the idea behind the title needs clarification at the outset, lest it prove to be seductive and therefore misleading. I suppose every one of us would like to be an astonishing preacher— unlikely though that seems on a week-to-week basis. But the plain fact is that no preacher can ever be astonishing (in a positive sense!) unless she has first been astonished. And the only regular and fully reliable source of astonishment for the Christian preacher is Scripture itself. Therefore, my aim in these first three chapters is to explore the Old Testament as a perpetual source of astonishment and, moreover, to consider how it is that we as preachers can put ourselves in the way of that astonishment, so as to be overtaken by it. Because so much theological work necessarily proceeds by the *via negativa*, I shall in each of the next three chapters identify some way of thinking about the biblical text that in my judgment impedes the flow of astonishment from the text to the preacher and, through the preacher, to the congregation.

I begin by contrasting two ways of viewing the Old Testament. The first I take to be common in the church, because it is the view with which most of my students seem to begin their theological study. Its essence is this: the Old Testament stands at an immense distance from us. As twenty-first-century readers, but even more as Christians, we view the text across a gulf that is wide and deep—historically, linguistically, morally, theologically. The distance discourages all but the boldest preachers. Occasionally, however, a preacher may venture across that gulf and bring something back: a nugget, a small treasure, that is congenial with the gospel message and adds to it sparkle or depth of background.

This book holds up a tradition of reading and preaching the Old Testament that sees matters very differently. When I say "tradition," I am speaking loosely. The people upon whom I draw are scattered through the centuries; they are in both the Eastern and the Western churches, and in several denominations in the West. But the crucial thing they share, and that distinguishes their view from the one I have just outlined, is that all of them experience the Old Testament as an *immediate presence* that exercises shaping force in Christian lives—indeed, that serves as a source of salutary pressure on our lives. Therefore, they view the Old Testament as a whole (and not just small nuggets of it) as indispensable for Christian theology and preaching.

It is crucial to understand that the difference between these two approaches has nothing to do with whether one has an awareness of historical criticism, and an appreciation for it. While some of the people I cite in these essays lived, died, and went on to glory entirely innocent of the Documentary Hypothesis, it is noteworthy that an excellent description of the text's immediacy comes from Gerhard von Rad, whose commitment to (and command of) historical criticism is undisputed. In the winter semester 1965–1966, von Rad led a practicum in exegesis and preaching, along with his Heidelberg colleagues Günther Bornkamm and Hans Freiherr von Campenhausen—a dream team of modern biblical scholarship. These words are from von Rad's opening address to their students:

> The great discovery which all of you must make in preaching is that the texts themselves actually speak. . . . The best sermons are those in which one notes the preacher's own surprise that—and how—the text suddenly began to speak. I have heard sermons in which one had the feeling that the preacher only stepped a little to one side in order to let the text speak (now of course he had already done something more!). In the *Kirchenkampf* [the German church's struggle with the Nazi regime] I heard sermons in which the text slipped out of the preacher's hands and fell from the pulpit; it was so incredibly timely and pertinent that the preacher completely lost control over it. These may be extreme cases, but they are still better than trite, hackneyed Christian chatter. Good sermons have something of an intellectual adventure about them. I give you about ten to twenty beginners' sermons, in which you will repeat what you have learned. Then you will have preached yourselves out. Then if you do not make the discovery that every text wants to speak for itself, you are lost.[2]

Von Rad touches on three things that are fundamental to the approach to the text that informs my thinking here. First, when the text speaks, there is a surprise in store, and in the first instance, *the surprise is for the preacher.* "Good sermons have something of an intellectual adventure about them." When you choose a preaching text, you do not

---

2. Gerhard von Rad, *Biblical Interpretations in Preaching*, trans. John E. Steely (Nashville: Abingdon, 1977), 17–18. Brackets in original.

really know what you are getting into. You are entrusting yourself to the text. That means that as yet you have no sense (not, in my experience, until you are very deep into premeditating the sermon) of all that it has to say to you and through you on this particular occasion.[3]

A second and closely related point: the role of the preacher is to "step a little to one side" and let the text have its say. On this point, von Rad does not mince words: if you cannot get out of the way when the text is ready to speak for itself, then you are lost. Quite simply, you will find yourself with nothing to say—nothing of substance, that is, because the source of inspiration for the sermon is not the preacher but the text. You might say that the role of the preacher is to serve as "First Listener" to the text. You are the first one to listen to how the text is speaking on this occasion, at this point in world history, in this particular assembly of the body of Christ. But (thank God) you are not the only listener on this occasion. And if you succeed in bringing forward the text week after week and letting it have its say, then part of the surprise will be that others listening with you will hear parts of its message that you have missed. When that happens, you will know that you have done well. You have enabled them to learn something that many regular churchgoers never learn: that the Bible speaks with many different voices, that it represents a lively conversation—at times, a tension-filled argument. Only by listening closely to Scripture day by day and week by week do we learn to distinguish among those voices so that we no longer hear a dulling cacophony but rather a message that is complex, nuanced, and far from predictable.

Von Rad shares the view common to all the great premodern theological interpreters of Scripture: that the Bible is *essentially surprising* in all its parts and that as we discipline ourselves to listen to it carefully, our working assumptions about "the way things really are" change. Our world itself becomes a surprising place. *"Pay attention to what you hear; the measure you give will be the measure you get, and still more will be given you"* (Mark 4:24 NRSV). So the preacher whose own astonishment is perpetually renewed by what she hears will be the one who is able to engage in the sustained practice of "the art of astonishing."

---

3. Homiletician Eugene Lowry comments similarly: "The problem with preaching is that we have been trained to be answer people. . . . By the time we get ready to start preparing next Sunday's sermon we already know what we believe, and hence when we engage a text we often bring ourselves to the text rather than allowing the text to come to us. . . . The issue is how to get out of control, and the person who gets out of control is the one with the detective mindset, who is willing to be confused, willing to entertain chaos, willing to head in the wrong direction for something surprising to happen." Lowry, quoted in Marlis McCollum, "Shortage of Good Preachers Has Multiple Roots," *Newsletter* of the College of Preachers, Winter 2003, 4.

"The art of astonishing"—thus Jean Leclercq describes the work of Bernard of Clairvaux, the twelfth-century Cistercian, who must have been one of the most breathtaking biblical preachers of all time. Bernard's eighty-six sermons on the Song of Songs are a carefully crafted literary work, and they attest only indirectly to his pulpit style.[4] Nonetheless, Bernard's reputation for public persuasion suggests that what is said of his writing must have been equally true of his preaching: Bernard knew that "the art of writing is the art of astonishing."[5] But as I read Bernard, what strikes me is that he was himself one of the most astonished readers of all time. The words of Scripture are food and drink for Bernard. He "masticates" them, as the medieval monks often said, chewing every word, like a grain of spice, until it yields its full savor.[6] He chews slowly—very slowly; in his eighty-six sermons on the Song, he only gets up to chapter 3, verse 1! And at the same time that his analytical mind is "scrutiniz[ing] every detail" (Ps. 111:2) of Holy Writ, Bernard is completely intoxicated by what he is chewing. His writing is indeed astonishing, but not because he invents new modes of theological discourse. He doesn't. Rather, the form of his art is to weave the received words of Scripture into new patterns that are both beautiful and unexpected. Bernard practices his art by paying exquisite attention to what he hears in the text.[7] The value of his sermons on the Song of Songs as instruction for preachers is that he shows just how he reads, what it is that surprises him—the very first line of the Song, for instance: "O that he would kiss me with the kisses of his mouth!" Why does that passionate exclamation erupt out of nowhere, in "a beginning that is not a beginning"? And since the bride asks specifically for a kiss, why bother to mention the mouth, the normal organ of kissing?[8] These are the questions of a fully alert reader. Thus Bernard's sermons offer us a model of the preacher as a skilled reader who in turn teaches the congregation how to read, leading them word by word through his own

4. See Jean Leclercq, "Were the Sermons on the Song of Songs Delivered in Chapter?" introduction to *On the Song of Songs II*, by Bernard of Clairvaux, CF 7 (Kalamazoo, Mich.: Cistercian, 1976), vii–xxx.

5. Jean Leclercq, "The Making of a Masterpiece," introduction to *On the Song of Songs IV*, by Bernard of Clairvaux, CF 40 (Kalamazoo, Mich.: Cistercian, 1980), xxii.

6. Admonishing the faithful to "sing wisely" the words of Scripture, Bernard says, "The soul that is sincere and wise will not fail to chew the psalm with the teeth as it were of the mind, because if he swallows it in a lump, without proper mastication, the palate will be cheated of the delicious flavor, sweeter even than honey that drips from the comb." Bernard of Clairvaux, Sermon 7.5, in *On the Song of Songs I*, trans. Kilian Walsh, OCSO, CF 4 (Kalamazoo, Mich.: Cistercian, 1971), 41–42.

7. In a recent essay, Denys Turner makes the very important argument that precisely because Bernard chooses the form and rhetoric of the homily (rather than that of the medieval scriptural commentary) for his discourses on the Song of Songs, he does not de-eroticize the text, as do virtually all other monastic commentators. Indeed, by adopting the Song's passionate style for his own, Bernard produces a much deeper and more engaging reading than any of his predecessors. Turner, "Metaphor, Poetry, and Allegory," in *Reading Texts, Seeking Wisdom: Scripture and Theology*, ed. David Ford and Graham Stanton (Grand Rapids: Eerdmans, 2004), 202–16.

8. Bernard of Clairvaux, Sermon 1.5, *On the Song of Songs I*, 3–4.

amazed reading of the text.[9] It is an empowering model—teaching people how to read Scripture in depth, with fascination and multiple questions—and one that should be more widely adopted by preachers.

A third point in von Rad's statement" is the particular concern of this chapter: the text itself constitutes an assertive presence in the act of preaching. A passage that leaps out of the preacher's hands and into the room exerts pressure on our minds and hearts. The Bible as a whole is pushing us toward something, though its internal tensions witness to the complexity of its subject matter and therefore the inevitable uncertainty of our understanding at many points. The Bible is pressing us toward reconciliation with God (cf. 2 Cor. 5:19); at the upper limit, it even imagines true intimacy with God to be a possibility for us. And one of the chief reasons the Old Testament is indispensable to the Christian preacher is that it shows us, more clearly and consistently even than the New Testament, how fundamental is our propensity for alienation. It also shows us, over a long and complex history, the wide variety of forms in which alienation from God can manifest itself, not just in our hearts, but also in our political and religious and social institutions.

Sometimes the scriptural pressure toward reconciliation is felt as welcome guidance for the perplexed. At other times its intensity is excruciating. This is especially true with the Prophets, who remind us relentlessly that the relationship between God and ourselves is frequently confrontational. Sometimes the two covenant partners stand in total mutual opposition. Speaking for myself, it is emotionally harrowing to dwell on the Prophets. One of my students commented that the month we spent on them in the introductory Old Testament course was "almost unbearable"—and that suggests why Christian preachers need them. The prophetic insistence on the confrontational character of the relationship between God and ourselves is a salutary counter to the tendency of contemporary Christians to read the New Testament sentimentally and to overidentify with Jesus. "What would Jesus do?"—I suppose that is a good question for disciples to ask, as long as we also admit how little we are inclined to go and do likewise. The Prophets, indeed most of Israel's Scriptures, force us to admit that, precisely as religious people, we are very often self-deceived about our closeness to God. Thus God exposes that self-deception through the prophet Jeremiah: "Am I a God near-at-hand . . . and not [also] God at-a-distance?" (Jer. 23:23).

---

9. Cf. Roland Barthes: "The teacher is the one who learns and teaches nothing other than the way he learns." Quoted in Avivah Zornberg, *The Particulars of Rapture: Reflections on Exodus* (New York: Doubleday, 2001), 140.

UNCOMFORTABLE QUESTIONS

The pressure toward reconciliation begins very early in the Bible, already in the third chapter, where for the first time we see a verbal interaction between God and the newly minted human beings. It immediately becomes a confrontation, which proceeds by means of a series of increasingly uncomfortable questions posed by God: "Where are you? . . . Who told you that you are naked?" (Gen. 3:9, 11), and then an incredulous question, when it suddenly dawns on God what has happened: "From the tree—the one that I commanded you *not* to eat from it—you *ate*?" (v. 11). And then the tragically unanswerable question that God will pose to human beings over and over again, down through history to our own day: "What is this that you have done?" (v. 13).

What is striking about these questions is the degree to which they set Genesis apart from another "myth of origins" of which Israel surely knew, and to which the first chapters of Genesis are often compared, namely, the Epic of Gilgamesh. The two appear side by side in both freshman humanities and biblical studies courses, treated as early attempts to answer our perennial questions about the meaning of human existence, with its painful limitations. Yet when you look at what the Genesis story actually says, it is evident that there is a real difference from Gilgamesh. Genesis knows nothing about any sustained human quest for meaning. "The snake tricked me, and I ate" (v. 13); that is an accurate account of Eve's unpremeditated bid for knowledge. What we see in Genesis is Eve and Adam, not engaged in anything so noble as a quest, but merely going their own way, following the fancy of the moment. We see the familiar process of yielding to temptation, always with the rationale that if I want something badly enough, then somehow it must be good for me. So the tree is נֶחְמָד (*nehmad*), "*to be coveted* for making-wise" (v. 6). That word is suggestive; in Torah (including the Ten Commandments) the root חמד (*h-m-d*) most often refers to desire that is forbidden by God (Exod. 20:14 [17 Eng.]; 34:24; Deut. 5:18 [21 Eng.]; 7:25).[10] The One who is on a quest in this story is God, who seeks out the humans in hiding, presses upon them those uncomfortable questions, refuses to leave them alone with what the narrative elsewhere calls their "natural inclinations" (יֵצֶר לֵב הָאָדָם [*yetser lev ha'adam*], Gen. 8:21; cf. Gen. 6:5). Andrew Louth observes that the life, death, and resurrection of Jesus Christ disclose to us "the true character of mystery: mystery not just as the focus for *our*

10. The one exception is Gen. 2:9, although in that case the tree of life and the tree of knowledge are specifically excluded from the trees that God raises up as "נֶחְמָד (*nehmad*) to the sight and good for eating."

questioning and investigating, but mystery as that which *questions us,* which calls us to account."[11] Yet as Christians reading the Bible backward from the incarnation, we see that all along, from the beginning of the world (as Genesis tells it), the Divine Mystery has been calling radically into question our chosen *modus operandi,* our propensity for going our own way and thus going away from God. The scriptural witness to that questioning, so persistent throughout the Old Testament, is a source of pressure to which the preacher must respond.

At the same time, the biblical account is such that we cannot respond fully to that pressure without posing some questions of our own. A few chapters further in Genesis, with the story of the Binding of Isaac (Gen. 22), the narrative makes us so uncomfortable that we are compelled to ask questions about God. When I say that this story provokes questions about God, I am sounding like what I am: a twenty-first-century reader of the Bible. That is, I am already viewing the text from a certain perspective, and it is largely a contemporary one. We belong to a generation that struggles with the question of God's trustworthiness—or at least, with the trustworthiness of the biblical representation of God. We may think a story like this one would raise that question in every mind, but in fact, some of the most influential literature on Genesis 22 does not stumble at all over the scandal of what kind of God it is who would ask Abraham to offer up his son. Beginning with the Letter to the Hebrews, most Christian interpretations have focused instead on what the story says about the unswerving faith of Abraham: "He considered the fact that God is able even to raise someone from the dead" (Heb. 11:19 NRSV). Søren Kierkegaard's *Fear and Trembling,* surely one of the greatest articulations ever given to what Israel called יִרְאַת יְהוָה (*yir'at YHWH*), "fear of YHWH,"[12] likewise dwells on Abraham's "appalling" faith rather than on the problem of God.

But even if the classical Christian exegetical tradition is uninterested in the question of what this story has to say about God, that might still be a good question to ask. About any passage of the Bible there are better and worse questions to ask, and the preacher needs to know how to identify a fruitful question. There is, I think, only one criterion: a good question is one that leads you and your hearers more deeply into the story, not away from it and into pious abstractions—which may lean to

---

11. Andrew Louth, *Discerning the Mystery: An Essay on the Nature of Theology* (Oxford: Oxford University Press, 1983), 145. Italics in original.
12. For an excellent study of "fear of YHWH" in Genesis 22, see R. W. L. Moberly, *The Bible, Theology, and Faith: A Study of Abraham and Jesus* (Cambridge: Cambridge University Press, 2000).

the right or to the left but in either case fail to reflect the complex drama that unfolds through the biblical narrative. The better the question, the more it helps you attend to the particular words with which the story is told. "Listen to the words": this is the first and great commandment of reading and therefore of preaching the Bible, for that is how you will find the meaning of any good story (and the Binding of Isaac is a great piece of narration, in which not a word is waste). Its meaning is *in* the words, and not in some idea or "theme" the author sets floating about *behind* the words. Flannery O'Connor's astute observation about the wrong way to read fiction offers good warning and guidance also to readers and preachers of the Bible:

> People have a habit of saying, "What is the theme of your story?" and they expect you to give them a statement: "The theme of my story is the economic pressure of the machine on the middle class"—or some such absurdity. And when they've got a statement like that, they go off happy and feel it is no longer necessary to read the story. Some people have the notion that you read the story and then climb out of it into the meaning, but for the fiction writer himself the whole story is the meaning, because it is an experience, not an abstraction.[13]

Origen, the third-century theologian and preacher whose seminal and far-ranging scholarship established him as probably the most influential (Christian) Old Testament interpreter of all time,[14] likewise focuses attention on the words of the text. His remarkable sermon on Genesis 22 begins thus:

> Consider diligently how the faith of the faithful is proved from these words which have been read to us. . . . Observe each detail which has been written. For, if one knows how to dig into the depth, he will find a treasure in the details, and perhaps also, the precious jewels of the mysteries lie hidden where they are not esteemed.[15]

Although Origen is generally considered to be an uncompromising allegorist with no interest in the literal sense of the text, he preaches a

---

13. Flannery O'Connor, "The Nature and Aim of Fiction," in *Mystery and Manners*, by Flannery O'Connor, ed. S. and R. Fitzgerald (New York: Farrar, Straus & Giroux, 1969), 73.

14. See John David Dawson, *Christian Figural Reading and the Fashioning of Identity* (Berkeley: University of California Press, 2002).

15. Origen, *Homilies on Genesis and Exodus*, trans. Ronald Heine, FC 71 (Washington, D.C.: Catholic University of America Press, 1982), 136.

riveting account of the agonies Abraham endured during that three days' journey to the mountain with the beloved boy he fully intended to kill when they arrived.

Following that criterion of discovering the meaning of a story in its words, it is useful to ask what this one says about the character of God, because that question does receive some kind of answer from what the narrator and God say here. My experience with this particular story is that it yields meaning in tiny increments, a few words at a time. Although I had lectured and even written on Genesis 22, it was years before I heard what now seem to me to be the most important words in the chapter, when God says, "*Now I know* that you fear God, and you have not held back your son—your only one!—from me!" (Gen. 22:12). "Now I know"—if we assume that God really means that, then it suggests that this "testing" of Abraham (v. 1), grisly though it is, serves the ordinary function of a test: it is designed to determine something that cannot be known for certain any other way. "Now I know"—by means of this terrible test, and only by it, God comes to know whether there is any limit at all to Abraham's faithfulness.

And why is God's need to know so acute? The opening words of the story give the clue: וַיְהִי אַחַר הַדְּבָרִים הָאֵלֶּה (*vayhî ʾaḥar haddᵉvarîm haʾelleh*), "*And so it was, after these things,* that God tested Abraham." "After these things"—thus the narrator sends our minds back over the preceding events of Abraham's story in order to discover a reason and a warrant for this test. It is essential to find a warrant, if God is to be exonerated from the charge of arbitrariness that (in this case) amounts to sadism. The first reason, of course, is that at this point in history all God's eggs are in Abraham's basket. After the Tower of Babel debacle, God gave up on the direct approach to blessing the world; now it is only through Abraham and his seed that "all the families of the fertile soil" (Gen. 12:3) will experience blessing. So everything depends on Abraham's holding steady before God. But God's investment in him is at risk, because there is good reason to think that Abraham does not yet trust God wholeheartedly, reason to suspect that he may yet go his own way, as Eve and Adam did—as Abraham himself did in that highly unsatisfactory matter of twice passing Sarah off as his sister and letting her be taken into one or another royal harem to save his own skin. So this story astonishes, not only by revealing the depth of trust to which Abraham finally comes, but also by showing something of what covenant relationship means for God—namely, that God must likewise trust Abraham beyond any reasonable limit in order that the divine blessing of the world may not be lost.[16]

If the first commandment of biblical preaching is to listen closely to the words of the text, then the second is like unto it: Stop when you have said all that the words of Scripture and the basic grammar of Christian faith will support. The characteristic reticence of the biblical narrator means that there is much we cannot say with assurance about *why* God does what God does. Genesis unfolds Israel's astonishing conviction, unique in the ancient world, that the Most High God, Creator of heaven and earth, seeks profound, enduring relationship with human beings—and not just with one or two special individuals (as Israel's neighbors might concede) but with a whole family, even with "every living creature" (Gen. 9:12). Yet Genesis does not explain a lot of things we would really like to have explained. For instance, why does temptation exist in Eden? Why does God pick favorites (we call it "election")—like Abel, like Jacob—since it causes so much trouble? Or why—once it becomes clear that "the natural inclination of the human heart is evil from their childhood" (Gen. 8:21)—why doesn't God just scrap the whole batch and mix up a new one? The narrator rarely gives reasons, because the Divine Mystery is just that. Accordingly, the preacher's role is not to explain what cannot be explained; true mystery does not dissolve so easily, and we would be lost if it did.

It is the privilege of the preacher to orient people toward mystery, to lead them close enough to be touched by it. That is a priestly privilege, whether or not the preacher is formally ordained. And one thing that is evident from the biblical representation of priesthood is that it is a role that involves measured speaking; the presence of mystery reveals the foolishness of "trite, hackneyed Christian chatter" (von Rad). Therefore, the preacher must learn the discipline of reticence, of saying just enough for the language and the story of the Bible to become intelligible to those who listen, just enough for the distinctive voice of the text to be heard. If the preacher is practicing the discipline of reticence, then the result will be that week by week the congregation will experience the text as a real presence in its midst, a speaking presence whose promise and demand are increasingly comprehensible—and ultimately, convincing.

16. My three meditations on Genesis 22 are found in *The Art of Reading Scripture*, ed. Ellen F. Davis and Richard B. Hays (Grand Rapids: Eerdmans, 2003), 277–93.

UNCOMFORTABLE ANSWERS

If Christians are to be convinced by the biblical text, then they must know that the text not only speaks but also listens—indeed, that it can not only tolerate our uncomfortable questions but also respond to them, as I have implied in my treatment of Genesis 22. The point is crucial for contemporary readers, many of whom are rightly impatient with preaching and teaching that implies that reading faithfully is inconsistent with questioning the biblical account of God and ourselves: "God said it, I believe it, and that settles it." The writings of the twentieth-century theologian, preacher, and martyr Dietrich Bonhoeffer provide unusual insight into his experience of the biblical text as an immediate and active presence in the life of faith. This is the surprising paradox to which Bonhoeffer attests so clearly: the Bible is genuinely responsive to our sincere questioning, and yet its very responsiveness exerts pressure upon us. As we keep pressing our questions, the reciprocal pressure upon us builds. In the life of the most faithful (as Bonhoeffer himself experienced), pressure to respond to the God who speaks so directly to us amounts finally to coercion.

In April 1936, the thirty-year-old Bonhoeffer wrote a letter to his brother-in-law Rüdiger Schleicher about a question that was troubling both of them: "How can I live a Christian life in the real world, and where are the final authorities for such a life, which alone is worth living?" As his country was moving toward war, Bonhoeffer took charge of the "Preachers' Seminary" at Finkenwalde, where he lived in community with twenty-five young pastors-in-training for the Confessing Church. Schleicher, a lawyer who often served as Bonhoeffer's theological sparring partner, at that time took the liberal Protestant position espoused by Adolf von Harnack. Although Bonhoeffer had once been a student of Harnack's, his letter shows the outcome of the "momentous inner revolution"[17] that had occurred in his mind over the last few years:

> First, I want to confess quite simply that I believe the Bible alone is the answer to all our questions, and that *we only need to ask persistently and with some humility* in order to receive the answer from it. One cannot simply read the Bible the way one reads other books. *One must be prepared to really question it.*

17. The description is that of Eberhard Bethge, Bonhoeffer's intimate friend and biographer. See G. B. Kelly and F. B. Nelson, eds., "Bonhoeffer's Inner Liberation: Letters on Becoming a Christian (1935–1939)," in *A Testament to Freedom: The Essential Writings of Dietrich Bonhoeffer* (San Francisco: Harper & Row, 1990), 445.

Only then will it open itself up. Only when we await the final
answer from the Bible will it be given to us. That is because in
the Bible it is God who speaks to us. And we cannot simply reach
our own conclusions about God; rather, we must ask him. He will
only answer us if we are seeking after him. Naturally, one can
also read the Bible like any other book—from the perspective of
textual criticism, for instance. There is nothing to be said against
that. But that will only reveal the surface of the Bible, not what
is within it. When a dear friend speaks a word to us, do we subject it to analysis? No, we simply accept it, and then it resonates
inside us for days. The word of someone we love opens itself up
to us the more we "ponder it in our hearts," as Mary did. In the
same way, we should carry the Word of the Bible around with
us. We will only be happy in our reading of the Bible when we
dare to approach it as the means by which God really speaks to
us, *the God who loves us and will not leave us with our questions unanswered.*[18]

Bonhoeffer acknowledges that his new way of reading the Bible may
sound (and be) unsophisticated, and at the same time he confesses "how
happy one can be to find one's way back from the false tracks of so much
theology to these primitive things."[19] Yet we gain some perspective on
this "primitive" position of a young and passionate theologian living in
extreme times when we recognize that almost thirty years later von Rad,
arguably the most able Old Testament scholar of his generation, would
look back to the *Kirchenkampf* and articulate the same conviction for the
benefit of his young students: that the Bible is an urgent, speaking presence. Of course, von Rad survived into less extreme times, but he did not
become so "sophisticated" as to forget what the years of struggle had
taught: that wise readers of the Bible are those who are able to free themselves of what they think they already know and listen for the unexpected thing that God now has to say to them.

The essence of Bonhoeffer's hermeneutic is that God's word in Scripture must be heard and preached as command, and that command "now
requires something quite definite from us."[20] This may not seem to distinguish him from interpreters who use the notion of Bible-as-command

18. Dietrich Bonhoeffer, *Meditating on the Word*, trans. David Gracie (Cambridge, Mass.: Cowley, 2000),
34–35. Emphasis mine.
19. Ibid., 38.
20. See Bonhoeffer's 1932 paper "A Theological Basis for the World Alliance," in *No Rusty Swords: Letters,
Lectures, and Notes, 1928–1936* (New York: Harper & Row, 1965), 163.

in order to foreclose questioning. What does distinguish Bonhoeffer, and what makes his hermeneutic so compelling, is the fact that he heard the almost unbearable command of God directed first of all to—and against—himself. The "happiness" of moving away from false tracks of theology would cause him to forfeit more ordinary forms of happiness; it would take him to prison and ultimately cost him his life.

It was through reading the Prophets that Bonhoeffer most clearly heard God's command addressed to himself. From his student days in Tübingen, he was gripped by them, and especially by Jeremiah and Jonah, in whom he found the charter for his own experience of gradually losing his freedom in God's service.[21] In January 1934, when Bonhoeffer was pastor to a German congregation in London, he took a preaching text from Jeremiah, who gives unforgettable testimony to the experience of having his will entirely overpowered by God—and does not scruple to complain about it. Bonhoeffer chose a line from Jeremiah's most strident complaint:

> O LORD, you have enticed[22] me,
>   and I was enticed;
> you have overpowered me,
>   and you have prevailed.
> I have become a laughingstock all day long;
>   everyone mocks me.
>
> *(Jer. 20:7 NRSV)*

At that time, the German Evangelical Church was forming its alliance with the Nazi Party. In the course of the year, Bonhoeffer would lead German congregations in England to separate themselves from the Evangelical Church and join the newly formed Confessing Church. Now, under mounting pressure from Germany to stand behind the Reich bishop, what Bonhoeffer says of Jeremiah is transparent to his own growing sense of being divinely coerced:

> The noose is drawn tighter and more painfully, reminding Jere-
> miah that he is a prisoner. He is a prisoner and he has to follow.

---

21. Jonah is the subject of a poem Bonhoeffer wrote in Tegel prison in October 1944, when he was forced to give up an escape plan. His brother, his brother-in-law, and the legal advisor to the Confessing Church had all been arrested within a few days of one another, and Bonhoeffer realized that his "disappearance" would only bring his family into more danger. See *Dietrich Bonhoeffer: A Life in Pictures*, ed. Eberhard Bethge, Renate Bethge, and Christian Gremmels (Philadelphia: Fortress, 1986), 223.

22. The Hebrew word is פִּתִּיתַנִי (*pittîtanî*), which suggests seduction and (sometimes) deception. Although Bonhoeffer had studied Hebrew, he probably used the *Luther Bibel* (1912), which reads "Herr, du hast mich überredet, und ich habe mich überreden lassen." [Lord, you have talked me into (something), and I let myself be talked into it.]

His path is prescribed. It is the path of the man whom God will not let go, who will never be rid of God. . . .

He was upbraided as a disturber of the peace, an enemy of the people, just like all those, throughout the ages until the present day, who have been possessed and seized by God, for whom God had become too strong. . . . How gladly would he have shouted peace and *Heil* with the rest. . . .

The triumphal procession of truth and justice, the triumphal procession of God and his Scriptures through the world, drags in the wake of the chariot of victory a train of prisoners in chains. May he at the last bind us to his triumphal carriage so that, although in bonds and oppressed, we may participate in his victory![23]

The genius of Bonhoeffer's homiletical exegesis is that he has captured the complex of emotions—anguish, resentment, but also confidence in God—expressed by Jeremiah even as he sets his feet on the path prescribed. Bonhoeffer has at the same time drawn his twentieth-century audience into the drama of faithful witness to God's truth and justice: "May he at the last bind *us* to his triumphal carriage . . . !" The model of Jeremiah the bound prophet encouraged Bonhoeffer to stand against the church authorities of his own time. Jeremiah is of course literally bound by religious authorities; Pashhur, the chief priest at the temple, has him locked up in stocks. Later, Jeremiah is seized by his own countrymen and dragged off to exile in Egypt. But even more, Jeremiah is "possessed and seized by God"; he is one of the foremost prisoners in "the triumphal procession of God and his Scriptures through the world." The model of Jeremiah probably also helped Bonhoeffer accept the likelihood that he himself would participate in God's victory only on the far side of death: Jerusalem fell to the Babylonian army, just as Jeremiah said it would. The Third Reich fell, as Bonhoeffer had prayed and plotted that it should. But Jeremiah died in exile in Egypt, and Bonhoeffer was hanged in the Nazi camp at Flossenbürg on April 9, 1945.

Few preachers—almost certainly none of us—have been endowed with anything like Bonhoeffer's theological genius or his courage. It is doubtful that any of us will preach our way into martyrdom, as he did. But with our more modest gifts and in less dramatic circumstances, we may follow him—at a distance—in witnessing to the experience of

---

23. Quoted in Eberhard Bethge, *Dietrich Bonhoeffer: A Biography*, rev. and ed. Victoria J. Barnett (Minneapolis: Fortress, 2000), 346.

having our lives disrupted and profoundly changed by the word God speaks to us through Scripture. Like him, we are called to witness to the trustworthiness of God, and to make that witness convincing in situations that are always uncertain and sometimes desperately hard.

Bonhoeffer is able to offer reliable witness because, first, he hears God speaking through the medium of the text; second, he trusts God absolutely; and finally, he conforms his own words to what he hears. In the last analysis, perhaps every preacher faces the same challenge that Moses did at Meribah. All that we have to offer, to comfort the weary and frightened and lead them to God, are our words. Recall that at Meribah, Moses, embittered by the grumbling Israelites, spoke rash and foolish words: "Listen, you rebels, shall *we* [Aaron and I] bring water out of this rock for you?" (Num. 20:10). And he hit the rock. God's response was immediate and devastating: "Because you did not trust me enough to sanctify me in the eyes of the Israelites, therefore you will not bring this congregation into the land which I have given them" (v. 12). Generations of readers have struggled to pinpoint Moses' sin in this matter, but I know no better answer than this one, from a sixteenth-century Jewish commentator, the Maharal of Prague: trust in God can be nurtured only with words, not blows or anger.[24] We sanctify God in the eyes of others, we enable them to trust, by using words that clarify God's action rather than point to ourselves. Finding those words is the preacher's exacting task and, finally, her joy.

---

24. The Maharal is otherwise known as Judah Loew (1525–1609). This interpretation appears in his commentary on Exodus, *Gevurot ha-Shem*, ch. 7, cited in Zornberg, *Particulars of Rapture*, 242.

CHAPTER 2

Maximal Speech: Preaching the Psalms

Probably every preacher has one or two biblical books without which she feels she could not perform her ministry, let alone continue in a right faith from day to day—a book, or perhaps a small group of them, that is for her the richest source of preaching texts. Brevard Childs taught me to be suspicious of having "a canon within the canon," and as a teacher I try to be egalitarian—but not as a preacher. I unapologetically preach from the Psalter more than from any other book. That preference makes me somewhat unusual, and maybe distinctly odd among contemporary preachers. At one time preachers worked often from the book of Psalms, but that is no longer the case, and so I focus here on the peculiar virtues of the psalms as preaching texts.

In considering the question of why Christians do not preach more often and more robustly from the Old Testament, it is helpful to identify common impediments to such preaching—widely shared ideas or even inchoate feelings about the Old Testament in general that make it harder to reckon with a given text confidently and in depth. Having asked around a bit with respect to the psalms, I have come to the conclusion that the problem is, they are poetry. And for many of us, somewhere around tenth grade poetry ceased to be fun and began to be formidable, and it has remained so ever since. There is no point in minimizing the poetic character of the psalms; it is better to work with it. So part of what I want to suggest is that it is because each psalm is a well-crafted poem that they are endlessly interesting to preach—even fun to preach, although sometimes difficult fun.

However, the real reason I preach the psalms so often is that they break open my normally blinkered frame of reference and bring me, more quickly and fully than any other text, into the only frame of reference from which I might hope to speak a godly word. That is, they bring me into the story of Scripture—and my experience is not idiosyncratic. Indeed, they perform that service for all of us, if we read them in a state of spiritual alertness, and that is precisely why the psalms occur so frequently in the liturgy; in many traditions (including my own Anglican tradition), a psalm is read every time we gather for worship.

In order to see how this reorientation works, think about where the psalm appears in the order of worship: before the other Scripture readings, or at least before the Gospel. And we recite it together. Both its corporate recitation and its anterior position are clues to how the psalm brings us straight into Scripture. Because the Psalter speaks in the first person most of the time, it engages us directly in offering a prayer or a cry or a song to God: "O God, my God, it is for you I look first thing in the morning; my whole being thirsts for you" (Ps. 63:2 [1 Eng.]); "LORD,[1] how many enemies I have!" (Ps. 3:2 [1 Eng.]); "I exalt you, O LORD, because you lifted me up!" (Ps. 30:2 [1 Eng.]); "I love, because the LORD heard me" (Ps. 116:1). Putting the scriptural word directly into our mouths, these psalms assign us a distinctive voice—often a highly personalized voice—within the holy conversation that is our Scripture, and thus they give us a certain perspective from which to enter on any given day into the biblical story. For years I have prayed the psalms almost daily in corporate worship, yet only recently have I recognized that the position of the psalm within the order of service is already pointing to the best reason for preaching it. Coming immediately *before* the Scripture lessons or the Gospel, the psalm is meant to do the same thing the sermon should be doing immediately *afterward*—namely, helping us to be personally engaged with the biblical story.

Each worship service, with its Old Testament and New Testament readings, is a partial rehearsal of the entire biblical story, from creation to consummation. Participating day by day and week by week, we walk through that story of people we call our ancestors. Further, we learn to use the Scriptures as a map, so that we may locate our moment in history and even our own particular lives within that story. The psalm appointed

---

1. Here, as frequently, the psalmist uses the Tetragrammaton (YHWH). The sacred name of God is traditionally not pronounced in Hebrew, and yet the psalms beg to be read aloud. Therefore, I have rendered the Tetragrammaton as "LORD," as in most English translations. This word is, of course, also used as an exclamation in English. At times this added inference may be appropriate, as in the present instance.

for the day is something like the red X on the map posted at various stations along a hiking trail, advising the bewildered: "You are here." The psalm is orienting us—or reorienting us—every single day, and giving us a place to stand right now, in the church's prayers. And not just as individuals, of course. The psalm read at any particular service may or may not match our personal moods, and that is hardly the point. We are articulating that word of God, not just for ourselves individually, but for the whole body of Christ. The psalm is connecting us with the hope, the need, the spiritual insight of people whose experience, in some respects at least, differs vastly from our own. Putting time-tested words of prayer in our mouths, then, the psalm is offering us a place from which to move forward faithfully in the company of saints (big *S* and little *s*) who are journeying to God.[2]

The fifth-century monk John Cassian gives the best account I know of the special capacity of the psalms for drawing us out of ourselves and into the Scriptures. Thus he describes how the soul of the monk arrives at purity of prayer:

> [The monk] penetrates so deeply into the thinking of the psalms that he sings them not as though they had been composed by the prophet [David][3] but as if he himself had written them, as if this were his own private prayer uttered amid the deepest compunction of heart. Certainly he thinks of them as having been specifically composed for him and he recognizes that what they express was made real not simply once upon a time in the person of the prophet but that now, every day, they are being fulfilled in himself.
>
> Then indeed the Scriptures lie ever more clearly open to us. They are revealed, heart and sinew. Our experience not only brings us to know them but actually anticipates what they convey. The meaning of the words comes through to us not just by way of commentaries but by what we ourselves have gone through. Seized of the identical feelings in which the psalm was composed or sung we become, as it were, its author. We anticipate its idea instead of following it. We have a sense of it even before we make out the meaning of the words. . . . Instructed by

2. In his "Preface to the Psalter" (1528/1545), Martin Luther characterizes the Psalter as "the book of all saints. . . . For it teaches you in joy, fear, hope, and sorrow to think and speak as all the saints have thought and spoken." The "Preface" is reprinted in *Faith and Freedom: An Invitation to the Writings of Martin Luther*, ed. John Thornton and Susan Varenne (New York: Random House, 2002), 25–29. The quotation is on p. 28.
3. The early Christian writers generally spoke of the psalmist as "David" or "the prophet" (as prophesying Christ).

our own experiences we are not really learning through hearsay but have a feeling for these sentiments as things that we have already seen. They are not like things confided to our capacity for remembrance but, rather, we bring them to birth in the depths of our hearts as if they were feelings naturally there and part of our being.[4]

Cassian is describing what it is like to sing the psalms *from the inside*, to have them come out of our hearts and not just our mouths. The psalms become a sort of second nature to us—"we bring them to birth in the depths of our hearts as if they were feelings naturally there"—but, of course, second nature is something we acquire, through persistent practice. We get engaged with the psalms—and if I read Cassian correctly, getting engaged with the psalms is for him the first step in getting engaged with Scripture as a whole—we learn to feel the psalms by praying them, daily, over and over, so that they become a primary part of our "experience." Now Cassian is addressing monks, not preachers, but I think this is true for us as well. Not to put too fine a point on it: it is not possible to preach the psalms deeply and well unless you are also praying them regularly. All the great preachers of the psalms have first been prayers of them. I am thinking of Augustine and Calvin; I doubt that anyone has ever preached the psalms more deeply than they. From the seventeenth century, I think of John Donne. (His modern reputation is as a poet, of course, but Donne's contemporaries knew and valued him most as a preacher.) It was he who first introduced me to the preaching of the psalms, and he has influenced me in this more than any other.[5] Among twentieth-century preachers, I think of Dietrich Bonhoeffer and of Gardner Taylor, the 1976 Beecher Lecturer, who was justly proud of being a preacher from Brooklyn.[6]

All these preachers give evidence of reading the psalms from the inside, of reading with their hearts as well as their mouths and their intellects. In order to specify that style of reading, I identify three characteristics shared by those who preach the psalms well:

— First, they have learned how to think with the psalm, and even to feel what the psalmist feels. They can do this, as Luther points out,

---

4. John Cassian, *John Cassian: Conferences*, trans. Colm Luibheid, CWS (New York: Paulist Press, 1985), 137–38.
5. See my chapter on Donne in Ellen F. Davis, *Imagination Shaped: Old Testament Preaching in the Anglican Tradition* (Valley Forge, Pa.: Trinity Press International, 1995), 63–113.
6. See his lecture "Recognizing and Removing the Presumptuousness of Preaching," in *The Words of Gardner Taylor*, ed. Edward L. Taylor, vol. 5 (Valley Forge, Pa.: Judson, 2001), 147.

because the psalms give us not just a picture of the saints but their very words. We can share their vocabulary, their rhythms, their shouts of elation, and their groaning sighs.

—A second and closely related point: they take seriously the poetic character of the psalm, dwelling on its particular words and images, with patience and fascination.

—Third, they see each psalm not as a freestanding poem but as a structural element of the great cathedral that is the totality of Scripture. Scripture is for these preachers an exquisitely articulated edifice, which for all its complexity evidences also a comprehensive plan and unity. Therefore the primary context of the psalm is for them the Great Story that is the Christian Bible in both Testaments.

Each of these three characteristics of reading "from the inside" proves to be a strategy for discovering what it is in any given psalm that has the capacity for astonishing us.

INSTRUCTED EMOTION

First, then, these preachers have learned to think with—even *feel* with—the psalmist, so that praying a psalm is more like composing than reading. The key to that kind of deep prayer is to move slowly through the text, as if these thoughts and remarkably fresh words were coming into being for the very first time out of your own mind, your immediate encounter with God. Calvin aptly calls the psalms "An Anatomy of all the Parts of the Soul," because they teach us to see our own spiritual condition accurately.[7] This is the particular genius of the psalms: they instruct our feelings without negating them. They draw upon our particular experience of God as at the same time they expand it exponentially.

Like all poems, the psalms illumine something we might otherwise have missed, yet they make no attempt at explanation. They work by way of suggestion, not clear delineation. Since the psalmists, unlike many of their modern commentators, are not committed to linear thinking, there are countless leaps and switchbacks for which neither warning nor explanation is given. If we read too quickly, then, we may think that something has been left out, or maybe an editor put together two poetic fragments that don't really connect. Calvin is the great master at comprehending

---

7. John Calvin, *Commentary on the Book of Psalms,* trans. James Anderson (Grand Rapids: Eerdmans, 1949), 1:xxxvii.

the reasoning of both heart and mind that generated these poem-prayers, and his core insight is that the psalmists are not responding solely or directly to immediate circumstance. Certainly they register the pressure of the present situation; after all, a large proportion of the psalms are laments. Yet their response to trouble is based on something more fundamental than trouble itself, namely, on what they know to be true about God. A lamenting psalmist is "emotional," of course, but the emotions are those of second nature, of nature instructed by both faith and close observation of how God characteristically acts. Therefore, if we follow the words of these "saints" closely, we are in for some fruitful surprises.

On almost any page of Calvin's commentary, you can see the contrast between the psalmist's *theo*centric reasoning and our own thinking, which is very often uninstructed and therefore merely *ego*centric. Here is an instance from the Fifth Psalm, which begins as a strident lament. Three times the psalmist cries out for a hearing:

> Give ear to my words . . . ,
> pay attention to my moaning,
> listen to the sound of my screaming . . . ,
> because I am praying to you!
> *(Ps. 5:2–3 [1–2 Eng.])*

And then suddenly, there is that familiar yet still puzzling shift to a tone of confidence. While enemies are pressing in on every side, the psalmist says with perfect assurance:

> You will undo those who speak lies. . . .
> But as for me, by the abundance of your חֶסֶד (*ḥesed*; your
>   unshakable love),
> I will enter your house.
> *(Ps. 5:7–8 [6–7 Eng.])*

Calvin's comment is striking:

> The great object which David has in view, is to show, that since the cruelty and treachery of his enemies had reached their utmost height, *it was impossible but that God would soon arrest them in their course.* His reasoning is grounded upon the nature of God. . . . How is it possible for them to escape from his hand unpunished, seeing he is the judge of the world?[8]

---

8. Ibid., 1:55. Emphasis mine.

Calvin points to the stunning paradox that the psalmist is most confident just when the situation is most desperate. Our reaction is the opposite, of course: when wickedness is at its height and "God does not immediately restrain it, we are either stupefied and dismayed, or cast down into despair."[9] If we only understood, we would feel encouraged all the more "to send up our groanings to heaven, because God will not suffer their rage to proceed to the uttermost, but will bring forth their malice and wicked devices to the light."[10]

The psalmist goes on to pray, "Let them fall from their counsels" (Ps. 5:11 [10 Eng.]), and Calvin makes the accurate but hardly obvious observation that those who exercise worldly power often fall through their remarkable stupidity: "If we find those who desire to do us mischief to be clear-headed and sharp-witted persons, let us remember, that it is the continual office of God to strike with stupidity and madness those who are wise to commit iniquity."[11] To test that observation, you might think of a biblical example: Pharaoh's court magicians, in order to counter the divinely sent plagues, produce more blood, more frogs. It is the deluded exercise of Egyptian power that will bring down Egypt. In our own historical era, recall that the Nazi obsession with keeping trains running to the death camps was ultimately a significant factor in the fall of the Third Reich, for it meant that troops at the front were badly undersupplied.

In reminding us of the stupidity of the wicked, Calvin is speaking in the first instance to our fear, since the psalmist is a victim of the powerful. But we who preach in what is currently the world's most powerful country should remember that the psalm speaks differently to those who exercise power. In order to preach faithfully, then, we may need to turn it 180 degrees, so that the call for God's redress of evil may serve as a warning against our own temptation to godless arrogance.

PREACHING A POEM

The second characteristic I have identified in those who preach the psalms well is that they take seriously the fact that these are poems. George Steiner puts the matter succinctly: "A poem is maximal speech."[12] A good poet does not willingly waste a word, and certainly not

---

9. Ibid.
10. Ibid., 1:60.
11. Ibid., 1:61.
12. George Steiner, *After Babel: Aspects of Language and Translation* (New York: Oxford University Press, 1975), 233.

an image. The best way to prepare to preach a psalm is to read it over and over aloud, until you can see how and why one line yields to the next, until its images are haunting your imagination, until its phraseology and its particular pattern of repetition-with-variation (for that is the basic pattern of Israelite poetry) become distinctive in your mind.

One of the peculiar pleasures and even sources of confidence for the preacher is that when you choose a psalm as your text, you get to work with a complete literary composition—whereas in every other book, you are working with a fragment of a larger whole. A good preacher might pick out a single line that becomes the rhetorical focus of the sermon. Donne, for example, regularly does that. Yet if you examine each of his sermons carefully, you will see that he is working with the thought of the whole psalm.

Moreover, "a good poem . . . cannot be written or read in distraction," as Wendell Berry has said,[13] and that is the great value of the psalms as texts for our distracted age. You cannot skim them and preach the main idea, the gist of the thing. You have to dwell on the words, and the reward for doing so is a fresh view of the world. The gifted poet uses words to yield a changed perception of what we cavalierly call "reality," as though that were a fixed quantity. But more than that, the poet's words change us. The best poems persuade us to think and act differently. In his tribute to Yeats, W. H. Auden evokes the capacity of the great poet to change us:

> Follow, poet, follow right
> To the bottom of the night,
> With your unconstraining voice
> Still persuade us to rejoice;
>
> With the farming of a verse
> Make a vineyard of the curse,
> Sing of human unsuccess
> In a rapture of distress;
>
> In the deserts of the heart
> Let the healing fountain start,
> In the prison of his days
> Teach the free man how to praise.[14]

---

13. Wendell Berry, "The Responsibility of the Poet," in *What Are People For?* (New York: North Point, 1990), 90.

14. W. H. Auden, "In Memory of W. B. Yeats" (1939), in *W. H. Auden: Collected Poems*, ed. Edward Mendelson (New York: Random House, 1976), 198.

"Follow, poet, follow right / To the bottom of the night"—and out of that depth, "Teach the free man how to praise." Auden might be speaking to any of the Israelite poets who left us such a legacy of lament psalms in a book whose Hebrew title is תְּהִלִּים (*t*ᵉ*hillîm*), "Praises." The laments attest to the extraordinary range of emotional experience that underlies the words of those who have learned to praise God in freedom. Sometimes the psalmist's freedom before God is astonishing; it confounds all ordinary teachings about prayer. For instance, Psalms 39 and 88 are unremitting accusations directed against God's supposed forgetfulness, contempt, and enmity toward the faithful. In the former, the psalmist actually demands *less* of God's unwelcome attention:

> Turn your gaze from me, so I may show some cheer,
> before I go away and am no more!
> *(Ps. 39:14 [13 Eng.])*

What is the logic of that kind of prayer? These psalms give voice to a despair that is one degree short of absolute, and that one degree gives them a place in the book called "Praises," and in the life of those learning to praise God in freedom. Although he is speaking of a secular poem (Hayden Carruth's "On Being Asked to Write a Poem Against the War in Vietnam"), Wendell Berry's comment is apt:

> The distinguishing characteristic of absolute despair is silence. There is a world of difference between the person who, believing that there is no use, says so to himself or to no one, and the person who says it aloud to someone else. A person who marks his trail into despair remembers hope—and thus has hope, even if only a little.[15]

The psalmists, of course, are marking the trail into despair in God's plain sight, so that God can follow "to the bottom of the night" the one who is crying out in anguish. And that makes all the difference.

Sometimes it is not the sheer poetic quality of a line that generates a sermon but rather the way it brings to mind an unresolved theological question. From Psalm 51: "Wash me through and through from my wickedness" (v. 2 BCP [4 Heb.]). Now, what is the process by which God rids us of our sins? Do they really disappear, like spots before some metaphysical dry-cleaning agent, or is that just wishful thinking—especially

---

15. Wendell Berry, "A Poem of Difficult Hope," in *What Are People For?* 59.

when our sins have not only stained our own souls but also wrought drastic change, even permanent damage, in the lives of others? (Remember, Psalm 51 is traditionally associated with David's sins of adultery and murder.) It is telling that as this psalmist envisions the experience of forgiveness, it seems less like a divine operation *on* us than divine presence *with* us. Thus "David" pleads:

> Do not cast me away from [being] before you;
> And your Holy Spirit take not away from me!
>
> *(v. 13 [11 Eng.])*

We know forgiveness as God's "generous spirit" (v. 14 [12 Eng.])[16] finds an opening in us, when our own spirits and hearts break completely (v. 19 [17 Eng.]) and we are finally desperate enough to be "created anew" by God (v. 12 [10 Eng.]).[17]

The main reason to preach the psalms is not the bare fact that they contain great lines or great metaphors. Rather, it is because the poets who composed them thought differently about God than we ordinarily do, and more deeply. Nonetheless, my own work on a psalm does often begin with a line that will not leave me alone—Psalm 40:9: וְתוֹרָתְךָ בְּתוֹךְ מֵעָי (*vᵉtôratᵉkha bᵉtôkh meʿai*).[18] *The Book of Common Prayer* offers a somewhat pallid translation: "Your law is deep in my heart"; similarly, the NRSV (v. 8): "Your law is within my heart." But the Hebrew word מֵעָי (*meʿai*) means "guts," not "heart." Therefore, the New Jewish Publication Society's *Tanakh* is anatomically correct with "Your teaching is in my inmost parts," although the phrase is strained in English. Peter Levi, himself a poet and student of poetry, probably does the best job of any published translation: "[Y]our law is written in my body."[19] (Since the translation of poetry is always a vexed matter, preachers who do not read Hebrew are advised to compare translations of the psalms carefully.) But the Hebrew line is even leaner and more direct: "Your Torah is within my guts." God's sacred Teaching is given again; my body is a second Sinai; God's Holy Word and Writ are the fire burning in my belly. It is a generous God who gives a preacher a line like that to work with.

So in the sermon I stick with that stupendous line and consider what the world looks like through the eyes of this person living with Torah in

---

16. Psalm 51:14 [12 Eng.] is syntactically ambiguous. It may be translated either "With a generous spirit sustain me" or "Sustain in me a generous/willing spirit."

17. See my sermon on Psalm 51, "Voluntary Heartbreak," in *Getting Involved with God: Rediscovering the Old Testament* (Cambridge, Mass.: Cowley, 2001), 168–75.

18. See my sermon on Psalm 40, "Demanding Deliverance," in *Preaching from Psalms, Oracles, and Parables*, ed. Roger Alling and David J. Schlafer, Sermons That Work 14 (Harrisburg, Pa.: Morehouse, forthcoming).

19. Peter Levi, trans., *The Psalms* (London: Penguin, 1976), 61.

her guts. I see three things, all of them astonishing, when you slow down enough to think about it. First, as the psalmist prays:

O Lord my God, your wonders
and your thoughts—they are toward us!
(Ps. 40:6 [5 Eng.])

God is thinking "to-usward," as Miles Coverdale put it in his wonderfully vivid sixteenth-century translation of the Psalter, the first rendering in English. God, Creator of heaven and earth, is thinking about us—a lot, if you believe Torah (the Pentateuch) and the Prophets. If indeed that is so, then it means that prayer is something other than self-delusion. Rather, prayer is sending our thoughts, our longings and intentions and praise, back along the same pathways by which God's thoughts have already traveled to-usward.

A second surprising inference: this psalm is a strong lament, and therefore it seems that the person who holds Torah in his guts is characterized, not by self-confidence (as you might expect), but by its opposite, namely, conscious helplessness and utter dependence on God. This idea makes perfect sense when you think about the two biblical figures who tell us that they actually ate God's Word: Jeremiah and Ezekiel (Jer. 15:16; Ezek. 3:1–3). Make of that consumption what you will—metaphor or sign act—those prophets testify that once they had eaten Torah, their lives were totally out of their own control.

Related to the element of conscious helplessness is the third inference I draw from this psalm. Living with Torah in your guts means living with raw, unrelieved expectation, for that is the sustained tone of this psalm. Its final line is "My God! Don't be slow!" The psalmist knows what God has done and therefore what God has yet to do; she is burning to see God act for deliverance and healing in her own life and in our groaning world. The note of longing, of eager expectation, is pronounced in this psalm and in the Psalter altogether. The common translation of the first line misleadingly downplays that tension: "I waited patiently for the Lord." קַוֹּה קִוִּיתִי (*qavvoh qivvîtî*)—"I waited on tenterhooks" is more like it. The monastic theologians of the Middle Ages, who prayed right through the Psalter (usually weekly), were attuned to that note of expectation. Accordingly, desire was the affect that seemed to them most pronounced in the Old Testament—and not because those monks were hopelessly sexually and socially repressed. Rather, through prayer they had come to share the biblical conviction, expressed so often in the Psalms and the Prophets and above all in the Song of Songs, that because intense longing for the things of God is part of our God-given nature, our longing will not, in the end, be disappointed.[20]

PREACHING WITHIN THE GREAT STORY

The third characteristic of preachers who read the psalms "from the inside" is that they treat the psalms within the context of the larger scriptural story. I have already alluded to how this functions in my own preaching: Psalm 40 sounds to me like a psalm that Ezekiel or Jeremiah might have written, and thinking about them in conjunction with the psalm gives me a better picture of what it's like to have Torah burning in your guts. That same instinct to connect a psalm with biblical narrative is of course what generated the superscriptions linking some psalms with David's life history, and in a few instances with Moses (Ps. 90) or Solomon (Pss. 72, 127). To my Christian imagination, proper linkage is not confined to the Old Testament. I recently preached Psalm 62, a psalm about waiting on God, and it reminded me for all the world of Mary the mother of Jesus, a potent biblical model of patience. So behind a psalm about waiting on God, I see the figure of Mary, waiting (you might say) with an intense patience for God's mysterious purpose to be worked out through faithful human life, suffering, and death—her own and her son's.

What I am suggesting is that the psalms have nearly inexhaustible potential for making connections with the larger biblical story. This relieves the preacher of the anxiety that has become a modern trademark of the profession, namely, the perceived need to "find an illustration," on which the success of the sermon is often supposed to depend. That is a pernicious idea, for very often the illustration proves to be the tail that wags the dog of the sermon (and I use that last phrase advisedly). But if you make good use of the narrative potential of the psalms, then you will be led naturally to illustrations that are appropriately subordinate to the psalm text.

Precisely because the psalms are not bound within a narrative, they can be recontextualized in a variety of narratives, including the stories of our own individual lives, or the corporate life of our congregation, or the nations.[21] If the psalms are to be genuine prayers for us, then we must make that effort of recontextualization and link them to our own concerns. That is why, when I teach the psalms, I always ask my students to

---

20. Jean Leclercq, *The Love of Learning and the Desire for God: A Study of Monastic Culture* (New York: Fordham University Press, 1982), 79–86.

21. See Brevard S. Childs, *Introduction to the Old Testament as Scripture* (Philadelphia: Fortress, 1979), 520–22.

keep a prayer journal. Yet in preaching, as in prayer, we should be wary of laying exclusive claim to the psalmist's persistent "I." No preacher's life can stretch big enough to fit every psalm, nor can it possibly be interesting enough to warrant such totalitarianism. For years I taught that the superscriptions that evoke events in David's life are meant to help us make an accurate linkage between the psalmist's words and our own stories, but I am now convinced that is only half their function. Equally, the allusions to David's story are raising our sights above and beyond our own little stories. They are guiding our imaginative entrée into the larger story of Scripture, for that is ultimately more edifying for our hearers. But even a biblical illustration should remain subordinate to the text at hand. That is, the biblical illustration should not overshadow the words of the psalm. Often the best illustration is no more than a thumbnail sketch, a reference to a familiar biblical character whose story illumines a particular point, and you can lay that out in a sentence or two.

I shall demonstrate this last point and conclude by turning to a sermon that, in my judgment, evidences with maximal effectiveness all three characteristics I have set forth as belonging to those who read and preach the psalms from the inside. On January 29, 1626, at St. Paul's Cathedral in London, John Donne preached on Psalm 63:7: "Because thou hast been my help, therefore in the shadow of thy wings will I rejoice" (KJV [8 Heb.]). Preachers should work carefully through the whole sermon, which just may be the most artful sermon on a psalm ever preached in the English language.[22] And while Donne is a literary genius, he is not wholly inimitable; there are multiple facets of his homiletical art that we ordinary mortals can incorporate into our own sets of preaching skills. Here I will focus on one of those: how Donne relates the psalm, first, to the larger story of Scripture, and second, to his own life and the lives of his hearers. And the crucial thing to note is that that order is important. We might expect Donne to begin with himself, because we modern preachers so often do—and also because (as his erotic poetry well attests), Jack Donne, the youthful London rake, had a strident ego, and his personality did not change when he eventually became Dr. Donne, dean of St. Paul's Cathedral. In fact, there is a strong personal element to his preaching, as also to his religious verse.[23] Yet

---

22. The text of the sermon follows, pages 33–61 of this volume.

23. John Carey makes the important point that the sermons and the poems need to be read together in order to understand "the distinctive structure of Donne's imagination." Carey, *John Donne: Life, Mind, and Art* (London: Faber & Faber, 1990), x. Unfortunately, Carey shows no understanding of the genuinely religious element of Donne's imagination and misreads the sermons as demonstrating merely a rhetoric of power. A much more plausible account of what motivates his preaching is offered in the excellent study by David L. Edwards, *John Donne: Man of Flesh and Spirit* (London: Continuum, 2001).

what breathes through all Donne's sermons is a subjectivity fundamentally re-formed by Scripture.

The Bible is for Donne a literary and theological unity, in which every component is integrally and artfully related to every other component, through the work of the Holy Spirit. So, taking his clue from the superscription, he naturally begins by setting the psalm within the narrative of David's life. "Of David, when he was in the wilderness of Judah"—David, being banished from Jerusalem, suffers political exile and in addition the most painful and dangerous affliction the churchman Donne can imagine, exile from the community of faith. Therefore, he launches into an extended meditation on both temporal and spiritual affliction. His audience would have had plenty of experience of both. As for temporal affliction, the immediately preceding year, 1625, had been a plague year in London.[24] But Donne has a special sensitivity to the experience of spiritual affliction. With remarkable insight, he perceives that God has let loose in his age "a new spiritual disease": religious indifference, skepticism, and an accompanying widespread spirit of sadness. Almost four centuries later, we can say that religious indifference is the disease of modernity, yet we must recall that no generation of Europeans had seen it before Donne.

Like any preacher, Donne is eager to address the needs of the moment, and the way he does that is to show how variously and deeply Scripture speaks to the conditions of both kinds of affliction. Beginning with David, he briefly reviews the (biblical) histories of many who suffered much and yet clung to God: Jeremiah, Susanna, Joseph, Job, the persecuted Christ. The result is that when Donne finally takes up the psalmist's "I" and speaks in the first person, it is a comprehensive "I," not confined to the experiences of the preacher or even the totality of his immediate audience. He is bringing to bear a perspective that could not be gained by an individual or a single generation, for it is based on the long, multivoiced, and therefore reliable witness of Scripture. Having heard that witness at length, we can trust Donne when he assures us that temporal suffering—loss of health, reputation, fortune—is endurable, and not ultimately fearful: "If God withdraw not his spiritual blessings, his grace, his patience—if I can call my suffering his doing, my passion his action—all this that is temporal is but a caterpillar got into one corner of my garden, but a mildew fallen upon one acre of my corn. The body of all, the substance of all is safe, as long as the soul is safe."[25]

24. George Potter and Evelyn Simpson, introduction to *The Sermons of John Donne*, vol. 7, ed. George Potter and Evelyn Simpson (Berkeley: University of California Press, 1954), 1.
25. John Donne, Sermon on Psalm 63:7, in Potter and Simpson, *Sermons of John Donne*, 7:56.

We can trust Donne further when he shows us "the fearful depth" of spiritual misery—when he does the most difficult and risky thing any preacher can do, trying to get us, his hearers, to see ourselves for what, in one aspect, we are: the enemies of God. And he shows that even in that situation of complete alienation, we are still utterly dependent on the mercy of God, and not hopeless of receiving it. (I suggest that you read the following aloud, and as you listen, notice that Donne's preaching often becomes prayer, like the psalms, addressed directly to God.)

> When I shall need peace—because there is none but thou, O Lord, that should stand for me—and then shall find that all the wounds that I have come from thy hand, all the arrows that stick in me, from thy quiver; when I shall see that because I have given myself to my corrupt nature, thou hast changed thine, and because I am all evil towards thee, therefore thou hast given over being good towards me; when it comes to this height, that . . . mine enemy is not an imaginary enemy, fortune, nor a transitory enemy, malice in great persons, but a real and an irresistible and an inexorable and an everlasting enemy, the Lord of Hosts himself, the Almighty God himself—the Almighty God himself only knows the weight of this affliction, and except he put in that *pondus gloriae*, that exceeding weight of an eternal glory, with his own hand into the other scale, we are weighed down, we are swallowed up, irreparably, irrevocably, irrecoverably, irremediably.[26]

Donne means to sober us, yet he does not leave the matter with that terrible uncertainty. "Because thou hast been my help, therefore in the shadow of thy wings *will I rejoice*." The psalm passes through misery but, remembering God's faithfulness in the past, looks to future joy. And so does Donne's sermon. Because he himself struggled long and deeply with dejection, he often preaches directly to it. Donne knew death well (by the time this sermon was preached, he had lost his adored wife, Ann, and five of the twelve children born to them),[27] and he reckons with it squarely in sermon after sermon. Indeed, what makes his preaching so persuasive is precisely his realism about suffering and death, combined with his unshakable trust in the mercy of God, his conviction that God

---

26. Ibid., 7:56–57.
27. Of the twelve children born to Ann and John, ten survived birth. By 1626, three more had died, and a sixth, Lucy, died in January 1627, just after her eighteenth birthday. The rest outlived their father. Edwards, *John Donne*, 264, 275.

can and will deliver us from eternal death. Both in realism and in trust, Donne echoes his favorite biblical writers, the psalmists and the Apostle Paul—and in one other thing as well. Like the psalmists and Paul, the preacher Donne repeatedly enjoins us to rejoice in what is good in this world, even as we look to what God yet has to do. He ends his sermon by training his imagination on one of his favorite subjects, heaven and his own anticipated joy in it:

> Howling is the noise of hell; singing the voice of heaven. Sadness the damp of hell; rejoicing the serenity of heaven. And he that hath not this joy here lacks one of the best pieces of his evidence for the joys of heaven, and hath neglected or refused that earnest by which God uses to bind his bargain, that true joy in this world shall flow into the joy of heaven as a river flows into the sea. This joy shall not be put out in death and a new joy kindled in me in heaven. . . . (For all the way to heaven is heaven. And as those angels which came from heaven hither bring heaven with them and are in heaven here, so that soul that goes to heaven meets heaven here. . . .) As my soul shall not go towards heaven but go by heaven to heaven, to the heaven of heavens, so the true joy of a good soul in this world is the very joy of heaven. And we go thither, not that being without joy we might have joy infused into us, but that, as Christ says, "our joy might be full" (John 16:24), perfected, sealed with an everlast-ingness. For as he promises that "no man shall take our joy from us" (v. 22 GB), so neither shall Death itself take it away, nor so much as interrupt it or discontinue it. But as in the face of Death, when he lays hold upon me, and in the face of the devil, when he attempts me, I shall see the face of God (for everything shall be a glass, to reflect God upon me), so in the agonies of death, in the anguish of that dissolution, in the sorrows of that valediction, in the irreversibleness of that transmigration, I shall have a joy which shall no more evaporate than my soul shall evaporate—a joy that shall pass up and put on a more glorious garment above and be joy super-invested in glory. Amen.[28]

---

28. Donne, Sermon on Psalm 63:7, in Potter and Simpson, *Sermons of John Donne*, 7:70–71.

John Donne

The second of my Prebend Sermons upon my five psalms, preached at St. Paul's [Cathedral, London], January 29, 1625 [1626][1]

Because thou hast been my help,
therefore in the shadow of thy wings will I rejoice.

Ps. 63:7[2]

The psalms are the manna of the church. As manna tasted to every man like that that he liked best (Wis. 16:20[–21]),[3] so do the psalms minister instruction and satisfaction to every man in every emergency and occasion. David was not only a clear prophet of Christ himself but a prophet of every particular Christian. He foretells what I, what any shall do, and suffer, and say. And as the whole book of Psalms is *oleum effusum* (as the spouse speaks of the name of Christ; Song 1:3),[4] an ointment poured out upon all sorts of sores, a cerecloth[5] that supples[6] all bruises, a balm that searches all wounds, so are there some certain psalms that are imperial psalms that command over all affections and spread themselves over all occasions—catholic, universal psalms that apply themselves to all necessities. This is one of those, for of those Constitutions which are called Apostolic, one is that the church should meet every day to sing this psalm.[7] And accordingly, St. Chrysostom testifies that it was decreed and ordained by the primitive Fathers that no day should pass without the public singing of this psalm.[8] Under both these obligations (those

1. Until the eighteenth century, New Year's Day in England was March 25 (Lady Day, the Feast of the Annunciation). Therefore, dates that fall between January 1 and March 25 are reckoned one year earlier in the original ("old style") dating than in modern ("new style") dating. By the calendar in use in Donne's day, this sermon was delivered on January 29, 1625; by modern reckoning, the year was 1626. The basic text for the sermon as presented here is found in George Potter and Evelyn Simpson's monumental critical edition of all Donne's preserved sermons, *The Sermons of John Donne*, 10 vols. (Berkeley: University of California Press, 1953–1962), 7:51–71. The orthography has been modernized so that readers may "hear" the sermon with greater acuity.

2. Scripture references in the sermon follow the English versification. Except where otherwise noted, Donne's quotations and near quotations of Scripture in English follow the 1611 Authorized (King James) Version. Citations not supplied by Donne himself are enclosed in brackets. For extensive documentation of Donne's sources, both biblical and nonbiblical, see the critical edition of the Prebend sermons by Janel M. Mueller, *Donne's Prebend Sermons* (Cambridge, Mass.: Harvard University Press, 1971).

ancient Constitutions called the Apostles' and those ancient decrees made by the primitive Fathers) belongs to me, who have my part in the service of God's church, the especial meditation and recommendation of this psalm. And under a third obligation too: that it is one of those five psalms the daily rehearsing whereof is enjoined to me by the Constitutions of this church, as five other are to every other person of our body.[9] As the whole book is manna, so these five psalms are my *gomer*,[10] which I am to fill and empty every day of this manna.

Now as the spirit and soul of the whole book of Psalms is contracted into this psalm, so is the spirit and soul of this whole psalm contracted into this verse. "The key of the psalm" (as St. Jerome calls the titles of the psalms) tells us that David uttered this psalm "when he was in the wilderness of Judah." There we see the present occasion that moved him. And we see what was passed between God and him before, in the first clause of our text: "Because thou hast been my help." And then we see what was to come, by the rest: "Therefore in the shadow of thy wings will I rejoice." So that we have here the whole compass of time: past, present, and future. And these three parts of time shall be at this time the three parts of this exercise:[11] first, what David's distress put him upon for the present, and that lies in the context; secondly, how David built his assurance upon that which was past ("Because thou hast been my help"); and thirdly, what he established to himself for the future ("Therefore in the shadow of thy wings will I rejoice"). First, his distress in the wilderness, his present estate, carried him upon the memory of that which God had done for him before, and the remembrance of that carried him upon that of which he assured himself

3. ". . . [T]hou feddest thine own people with angels' food, . . . able to content every man's delight, and agreeing to every taste. For thy sustenance . . . tempered itself to every man's liking" (Wis. 16:20–21). Except where otherwise indicated, Scripture quotations in the notes are from the KJV.

4. "Your name is oil poured out [*oleum effusum*]" (Song 1:3 AT; the citations of Scripture in Latin generally follow the Vulgate). Donne, like virtually all premodern Christians, understood the Song of Songs as celebrating the love between Christ the bridegroom and the church as his bride.

5. cerecloth—a waxed cloth used for wrapping a dead body.

6. supples—softens (a wound) or eases (a swelling) by the application of ointment.

7. "When thou instructest the people, O bishop, command and exhort them to come constantly to church morning and evening every day . . . singing psalms and praying in the Lord's house: in the morning saying the sixty-second Psalm [63 Eng.], and in the evening the hundred and fortieth." *Apostolic Constitutions* 2.59 (*ANF* 7:422–23; cf. PG 1:744).

8. John Chrysostom, *Exposition of Psalm 140* (PG 55:427–28).

9. At St. Paul's, each of the thirty "prebends" (canons or other members of the cathedral chapter) was assigned a group of five psalms to recite on a daily basis. Thus they observed the monastic ideal of full recitation of the 150 psalms each day.

10. *gomer*—an approximate transliteration of the Hebrew word עֹמֶר (*'omer*), a dry measure. This was the quantity of manna that each Israelite was allowed to gather and consume daily (cf. Exod. 16:16–22).

11. Donne customarily opened each sermon by giving his audience an outline of what was to come, often using three major divisions. This was an aid to attention and memory, since he preached for an hour.

after. Fix upon God anywhere and you shall find him a circle.[12] He is with you now when you fix upon him; he was with you before, for he brought you to this fixation; and he will be with you hereafter, for "He is yesterday, and today, and the same for ever" (Heb. 13:8 BB).

12. The circle is Donne's favorite geometric figure, a symbol of continuity and wholeness.

For David's present condition, who was now in a banishment, in a persecution in the wilderness of Judah (which is our first part), we shall only insist upon that which is indeed spread over all the psalm to the text, and ratified in the text:[13] that in all those temporal calamities David was only sensible of his spiritual loss. It grieved him, not that he was kept from Saul's court, but that he was kept from God's church. For when he says by way of lamentation that he was "in a dry and thirsty land where no water was" (v. 1), he presses what penury, what barrenness, what drought and what thirst he meant: "to see thy power and thy glory, so as I have seen thee in the sanctuary" (v. 2). For there, "my soul shall be satisfied as with marrow and with fatness" (v. 5), and there, "my mouth shall praise thee with joyful lips" (v. 5). And in some few considerations conducing to this—that spiritual losses are incomparably heavier than temporal, and that therefore the restitution to our spiritual happiness (or the continuation of it) is rather to be made the subject of our prayers to God, in all pressures and distresses, than of temporal—we shall determine that first part. And for the particular branches of both the other parts (the remembering of God's benefits past and the building of an assurance for the future upon that remembrance), it may be fitter to open them to you anon, when we come to handle them, than now. Proceed we now to our first part, the comparing of temporal and spiritual afflictions.

13. Donne points to the fact that the whole psalm, including the single line that constitutes his preaching text, expresses an acute sense of spiritual loss.

PART I—DAVID'S PRESENT
CONDITION: AFFLICTION

Universal Affliction

In the way of this comparison falls first the consideration of the universality of afflictions in general and the inevitableness thereof. It is a blessed metaphor that the Holy Ghost hath put into the mouth of the Apostle: *pondus gloriae*,[14] that our afflictions are but "light" because there is "an exceeding and an eternal weight of glory" attending them (2 Cor. 4:17).[15] If it were not for that exceeding weight of glory, no other weight in this world could turn the scale or weigh down those infinite weights of afflictions that oppress us here. There is not only *pestis valde gravis* (Exod. 9:3)[16]—the pestilence grows heavy upon the land—but there is *musca valde gravis* (8:24).[17] God calls in but the fly to vex Egypt, and even the fly is a heavy burden unto them. It is not only Job that complains that he was "a burden to himself" (Job 7:20), but even Absalom's hair was a burden to him till it was polled (2 Sam. 14:26).[18] It is not only Jeremy that complains, *Aggravavit compedes* (Lam. 3:7),[19] that God had made their fetters and their chains heavy to them, but the workmen in harvest complain that God had made a fair day heavy unto them: "We have borne the heat, and the burden of the day" (Matt. 20:12). "Sand is heavy," says Solomon (Prov. 27:3). And how many suffer so—under a sand hill of crosses, daily, hourly afflictions that are heavy by their number, if not by their single weight? And "a stone is heavy" (says he in the same place)—and how many suffer so? How many, without any former preparatory cross—comminatory[20] or commonitory[21] cross—even in the midst of prosperity and security fall under some one stone, some grindstone, some millstone, some one

14. *pondus gloriae*—"a weight of glory." Although Paul is writing in Greek, he is probably engaging in conscious wordplay based on Hebrew, since the Hebrew word כָּבוֹד (*kavôd*) means both "weight" and "glory."

15. "For our light affliction, which is but for a moment, worketh for us a far more exceeding *and* eternal weight of glory" (2 Cor. 4:17).

16. *pestis valde gravis*—"an exceedingly heavy (serious) pestilence."

17. *musca valde gravis*—"an exceedingly heavy fly (infestation)."

18. polled—cropped (of hair).

19. "He hath made my chain heavy" (Lam. 3:7). Donne follows the tradition that Lamentations was written by the prophet Jeremiah.

20. comminatory—threatening (Latin, *comminor*).

21. commonitory—serving to warn (Latin, *commoneo*).

insupportable cross that ruins them? But then (says Solomon there), "a fool's anger is heavier than both." And how many children, and servants, and wives suffer under the anger, and morosity, and peevishness, and jealousy of foolish masters, and parents, and husbands, though they must not say so?[22] David and Solomon have cried out that all this world is "vanity" and "levity,"[23] and (God knows) all is weight, and burden, and heaviness, and oppression. And if there were not a weight of future glory to counterpoise it, we should all sink into nothing.

I ask not Mary Magdalene whether lightness were not a burden (for sin is certainly, sensibly a burden). But I ask Susanna[24] whether even chaste beauty were not a burden to her, and I ask Joseph whether personal comeliness were not a burden to him.[25] I ask not Dives,[26] who perished in the next world, the question. But I ask them who are made examples of Solomon's rule—of that "sore evil" (as he calls it): "riches kept to the owners thereof for their hurt" (Eccl. 5:13)—whether riches be not a burden.

All our life is a continual burden, yet we must not groan; a continual squeezing, yet we must not pant. And as in the tenderness of our childhood we suffer and yet are whipped if we cry, so we are complained of if we complain, and made delinquents if we call the times ill. And that which adds weight to weight and multiplies the sadness of this consideration is this: that still the best men have had most laid upon them. As soon as I hear God say that he hath found "an upright man, that fears God, and eschews evil" [Job 1:8], in the next lines I find a commission to Satan to bring in Sabeans and Chaldeans upon his cattle and servants, and fire and tempest upon his children, and loathsome diseases upon himself. As soon as I hear God say that he hath found "a man

22. Part of Donne's strong appeal as a preacher is his realism about the suffering that is a universal element of human experience, including the forms of suffering most common in his particular culture (here, the unexpressed and commonly unrecognized suffering of children, wives, and servants).

23. The Hebrew word to which Donne refers is הֶבֶל (*hevel*), which literally means "mist" and often connotes the insubstantiality, ephemerality, or absurdity of human life. See Pss. 39:6 [5 Eng.], 12 [11 Eng.]; 94:11; 144:4; Eccl. 1:2, 14; 2:1, 11, 15, etc.

24. Donne cites the deutero-canonical book by this name.

25. See Gen. 39:6–20.

26. The traditional Latin appellation for the "rich man" in Luke 16:19.

according to his own heart" [1 Sam. 13:14], I see his sons ravish his daughters, and then murder one another, and then rebel against the father and put him into straits for his life. As soon as I hear God testify of Christ at his baptism, "This is my beloved Son in whom I am well pleased" (Matt. 3:17),[27] I find that Son of his "led up by the Spirit . . . to be tempted of the devil" (Matt. 4:1). And after I hear God ratify the same testimony again at his transfiguration, "This is my beloved Son, in whom I am well pleased" (Matt. 17:5), I find that beloved Son of his deserted, abandoned, and given over to scribes, and Pharisees, and publicans, and Herodians, and priests, and soldiers, and people, and judges, and witnesses, and executioners. And he that was called the beloved Son of God and made partaker of the glory of heaven, in this world, in his transfiguration, is made now the Sewer of all the corruption,[28] of all the sins of this world—as no Son of God but a mere man, as no man but a contemptible worm.[29] As though the greatest weakness in this world were man, and the greatest fault in man were to be good, man is more miserable than other creatures, and good men more miserable than any other men.

Spiritual Affliction

But then there is *pondus gloriae*, an exceeding weight of eternal glory, and that turns the scale. For as it makes all worldly prosperity as dung, so it makes all worldly adversity as feathers. And so it had need, for in the scale against it, there are not only put temporal afflictions but spiritual too, and to these two kinds we may accommodate those words: "He that falls upon this stone" (upon temporal afflictions) may be bruised, broken, "but he upon whom that stone falls" (spiritual afflictions) "is in danger to be ground to powder" (Matt. 21:44).

27. Donne's observations here are a fine example of the critical reading of Scripture in the premodern period. It is noteworthy that Donne anticipates by several centuries Jon Levenson's argument that a reader who is attuned to the regular biblical pattern, beginning in Genesis, of favorite sons who suffer death (or deathlike experiences) should hear this pronouncement at Jesus' baptism as pointing to the passion. See Jon D. Levenson, *The Death and Resurrection of the Beloved Son: The Transformation of Child Sacrifice in Judaism and Christianity* (New Haven: Yale University Press, 1993).

28. The shocking image of Christ as the "Sewer of all . . . corruption" would have been all the more potent to Donne's London audience, because they were accustomed to seeing open cesspits all over the city—"some of them twenty feet deep and large enough for a man to drown in"; public toilets were often set up directly over these pits. See Francis Sheppard, *London: A History* (Oxford: Oxford University Press, 1998), 112.

29. Cf. Psalm 22:7 [6 Eng.]: "But I am a worm, and no man." Donne and his hearers would have seen the whole psalm as a witness to Christ's passion.

And then the great—and yet ordinary—danger is that these spiritual afflictions grow out of temporal: murmuring and diffidence in God and obduration out of worldly calamities. And so against nature, the fruit is greater and heavier than the tree, spiritual heavier than temporal affliction.

They who write of natural story[30] propose that plant for the greatest wonder in nature which, being no firmer than a bulrush or a reed, produces and bears for the fruit thereof no other but an entire and very hard stone.[31] That temporal affliction should produce spiritual stoniness and obduration is unnatural, yet ordinary.[32] Therefore doth God propose it as one of those greatest blessings which he multiplies upon his people: "I will take away your stony hearts . . . and give you hearts of flesh" (Ezek. 11:19; 36:26). And Lord, let me have a fleshly heart in any sense rather than a stony heart. We find mention amongst the observers of rarities in nature of hairy hearts, hearts of men that have been overgrown with hair. But of petrified hearts, hearts of men grown into stone, we read not. For this petrifaction of the heart, this stupefaction of a man, is the last blow of God's hand upon the heart of man in this world. Those great afflictions which are poured out of the vials of the seven angels upon the world (Rev. 16) are still accompanied with that heavy effect, that that affliction hardened them. "They were scorched with heats and . . . plagues" by the fourth angel, and it follows, "they blasphemed the name of God, . . . and repented not, to give him glory" (v. 9). Darkness was induced upon them by the fifth angel, and it follows, "they blasphemed the God of heaven, . . . and repented not of their deeds" (v. 11). And from the seventh angel there fell hailstones of the weight of talents (perchance four-pound

30. "Natural story" is what moderns would call "natural history."

31. That is, an entirely (thoroughly) hard stone. Here Donne seems to be drawing on the purported observations of the first-century Roman naturalist Pliny (see Pliny, *Natural History* 27.74, *lithospermon*).

32. Donne's observation about the unnatural hardening ("obduration") of the human heart is shrewd. From the perspective of biblical or Christian anthropology, especially as attested in many psalms, worldly affliction should naturally *break* our hearts, making us both more open to and more dependent upon God: "YHWH is near to the brokenhearted and delivers those crushed in spirit" (Ps. 34:19 AT [18 Eng.]; cf. Isa. 61:1).

weight)[33] upon men (v. 21). And yet these men had so much life left as to "blaspheme God" out of that respect[34] which alone should have brought them to glorify God, "because the plague thereof was exceeding great" (v. 21). And when a great plague brings them to blaspheme, how great shall that second plague be that comes upon them for blaspheming?

Let me wither and wear out mine age in a discomfortable, in an unwholesome, in a penurious prison, and so pay my debts with my bones, and recompense the wastefulness of my youth with the beggary of mine age.[35] Let me wither in a spittle[36] under sharp and foul and infamous diseases, and so recompense the wantonness of my youth with that loathsomeness in mine age. Yet if God withdraw not his spiritual blessings, his grace, his patience—if I can call my suffering his doing, my passion[37] his action—all this that is temporal is but a caterpillar got into one corner of my garden, but a mildew fallen upon one acre of my corn.[38] The body of all, the substance of all is safe, as long as the soul is safe.

But when I shall trust to that which we call a good spirit,[39] and God shall deject and impoverish and evacuate that spirit; when I shall rely upon a moral constancy, and God shall shake and enfeeble and enervate, destroy and demolish that constancy; when I shall think to refresh myself in the serenity and sweet air of a good conscience, and God shall call up the damps and vapors of hell itself and spread a cloud of diffidence and an impenetrable crust of desperation upon my conscience; when health shall fly from me, and I shall lay hold upon riches to succor me and comfort me in my sickness; and riches shall fly from me, and I shall snatch after favor and good opinion to comfort me in my

33. Although accurate information on biblical weights and measures was available in the seventeenth century, Donne seems to be guessing here. In fact, his estimate is far too low. The talent was the largest unit of weight, used for metals. In New Testament times, it seems to have been equivalent to about seventy-five pounds (*ISBE* 4:1054–55).

34. respect—consideration.

35. Here begins the first of two lengthy passages of the sermon in which Donne speaks in the first-person singular. (The second is the concluding passage.) There is real force to his adoption of the psalmist's first-person language here, because Donne's personal history is at several points reflected in this passage. He had come to see his own youth as "wanton"; he had often suffered from a "deject[ed] spirit"; he had been an ambitious young man who "snatch[ed] after favor and good opinion." Indeed, he had spent time in prison (for eloping with his employer's seventeen-year-old niece) and had subsequently spent many years, almost his entire married life, in poverty. So Donne speaks as a wise pastor who knows from the inside the desperation of the situations he cites and the weaknesses of the people he addresses.

36. spittle—hospital.

37. Many of Donne's hearers knew Latin, and so they would recognize that he uses the word "passion" (derived from the Latin *patior*) to denote both suffering and the passive experience of being acted *upon* by another (here, God). Both senses of the word are implied in the application of the word to Jesus' humiliation and crucifixion.

38. corn—here a general term for cereal grains.

39. This paragraph is one long sentence, through which Donne draws his audience down to "the fearful depth" of

poverty; when even this good opinion shall leave me, and calumnies and misinformations shall prevail against me; when I shall need peace—because there is none but thou, O Lord, that should stand for me—and then shall find that all the wounds that I have come from thy hand, all the arrows that stick in me, from thy quiver;[40] when I shall see that because I have given myself to my corrupt nature, thou hast changed thine, and because I am all evil towards thee, therefore thou hast given over being good towards me; when it comes to this height, that the fever is not in the humors but in the spirits, that mine enemy is not an imaginary enemy, fortune, nor a transitory enemy, malice in great persons, but a real and an irresistible and an inexorable and an everlasting enemy, the Lord of Hosts himself, the Almighty God himself—the Almighty God himself[41] only knows the weight of this affliction, and except he put in that *pondus gloriae*, that exceeding weight of an eternal glory, with his own hand into the other scale, we are weighed down, we are swallowed up, irreparably, irrevocably, irrecoverably, irremediably.

This is the fearful depth, this is spiritual misery, to be thus fallen from God. But was this David's case? Was he fallen thus far into a diffidence in God? No. But the danger, the precipice, the slippery sliding into that bottomless depth is to be excluded from the means of coming to God or staying with God. And this is that that David laments here: that by being banished and driven into the wilderness of Judah, he had not access to the sanctuary of the Lord, to sacrifice his part in the praise[42] and to receive his part in the prayers of the congregation. For angels pass not to ends but by ways and means, nor men to the glory of the triumphant church but

despondency and alienation from God. This extended sentence is more readily understood, and more moving, when it is read aloud.

40. Cf. Ps. 38:3 [2 Eng.]: "For thine arrows stick fast in me, and thy hand presseth me sore." In 1618, Donne preached a series of six sermons on this psalm. Addressed to the law students and faculty at Lincoln's Inn, London, where Donne had himself been a student some twenty-five years before, they are among the most personal and engaging of his sermons. See Potter and Simpson, *Sermons of John Donne*, 2:49–163.

41. The syntax of the sentence shifts subtly here, and Donne's theological point with it. "The Almighty God himself" identifies *both* "mine enemy," the source of affliction, and (immediately thereafter) the only source of deliverance.

42. "to *sacrifice* his part in the praise"—literally, to "make holy" by presenting offerings on the altar as well as by offering the prayers and songs of praise that constitute the Psalter.

by participation of the communion of the militant.[43] To this note David sets his harp in many, many psalms—sometimes, that God had suffered his enemies to possess his tabernacle: "He forsook the tabernacle of Shiloh . . . ; he delivered his strength into captivity, and his glory into the enemy's hands" (Ps. 78:60[–61]). But most commonly he complains that God disabled him from coming to the sanctuary. In which one thing he had summed up all his desires, all his prayers: "One thing have I desired of the Lord, that will I look after; that I may dwell in the house of the Lord all the days of my life, to behold the beauty of the Lord, and to enquire in his temple" (Ps. 27:4). His vehement desire of this he expresses again: "My soul thirsteth for God, for the living God; when shall I come and appear before God?" (Ps. 42:2). He expresses a holy jealousy, a religious envy even to the sparrows and swallows: "Yea, the sparrow hath found a house, and the swallow a nest for herself, and where she may lay her young, even thine altars, O Lord of hosts, my King and my God" (Ps. 84:3). Thou art my King and my God, and yet excludest me from that which thou affordest to sparrows—"And are not we of more value than many sparrows?" (Luke 12:7).

And as though David felt some false ease, some half-tentation,[44] some whispering that way—that God is "in the wilderness of Judah," in every place, as well as in his sanctuary—there is in the original in that place a pathetic, a vehement, a broken expressing expressed, "O thine altars" (Ps. 84:3). It is true (says David), thou art here in the wilderness and I may see thee here and serve thee here, but . . . "O thine altars, O Lord of hosts, my King and my God." When David could not come in person to that place, yet he bent towards the temple: "In thy fear will I worship towards thy holy temple"

43. Donne's audience would have known the phrase from the service of Holy Communion, in which the bidding for the prayers for the church reads: "Let us pray for the whole state of Christ's Church militant here in earth." It reflects an understanding of the Christian life that is central to Donne's own theology, namely, that in this world we are continually engaged in battles both temporal and spiritual.

44. tentation—inclination.

(Ps. 5:7); which was also Daniel's devotion: when he prayed, "his Chamber windows were open towards Jerusalem" (Dan. 6:10). And so is Hezekiah's turning to the wall to weep and to pray in his sick bed understood to be to that purpose: to conform and compose himself towards the temple (Isa. 38:2).[45] In the place consecrated for that use, God by Moses fixes the service and fixes the reward (Deut. 31:11).[46] And towards that place (when they could not come to it) doth Solomon direct their devotion in the consecration of the temple: "When they are in the wars, when they are in captivity, and pray towards this house, do thou hear them" (1 Kings 8:44[–49]). For as in private prayer, when (according to Christ's command) we are shut in our chamber,[47] there is exercised *modestia fidei*,[48] the modesty and bashfulness of our faith, not pressing upon God in his house, so in the public prayers of the congregation there is exercised the fervor and holy courage of our faith, for *agmine facto obsidemus Deum*,[49] "It is a mustering of our forces and a besieging of God." Therefore does David so much magnify their blessedness that are in this house of God: "Blessed are they that dwell in thy house, for they will be still praising thee" [Ps. 84:4]. Those that look towards it may praise thee sometimes, but those men who dwell in the church, and whose whole service lies in the church, have certainly an advantage of all other men (who are necessarily withdrawn by worldly businesses) in making themselves acceptable to Almighty God, if they do their duties, and observe their church services aright.[50]

Excommunication

Man being therefore thus subject naturally to manifold calamities, and spiritual calamities being incomparably heavier than temporal,

45. Cf. 2 Kings 20:2.

46. "When all Israel comes to appear before YHWH your God in the place that he shall choose, you shall read this Torah [Teaching] before all Israel, in their ears" (Deut. 31:11 AT).

47. See Matt. 6:6.

48. Tertullian, *Liber de Oratione* 1 (PL 1:1254–55; cf. ANF 3:681).

49. This appears to be a paraphrase of Tertullian, *Apologeticus adversus Gentes pro Christianis* 39 (PL 1:532).

50. The emphasis on duty indicates that Donne's comment on the "advantage" experienced by clergy who "dwell in the church" is more self-obligating than self-serving. (Similarly, see his opening comments on the daily recitation of psalms, pp. 33–34 above.)

and the greatest danger of falling into such spiritual calamities being in our absence from God's church, where only the outward means of happiness are ministered unto us, certainly there is much tenderness and deliberation to be used before the church doors be shut against any man. If I would not direct a prayer to God to excommunicate any man from the triumphant church (which were to damn him), I would not oil the key, I would not make the way too slippery for excommunications in the militant church.[51] For that is to endanger him. I know how distasteful a sin to God contumacy,[52] and contempt, and disobedience to order and authority is. And I know (and all men that choose not ignorance may know) that our excommunications (though calumniators impute them to small things, because many times the first complaint is of some small matter) never issue but upon contumacies, contempts, disobediences to the church. But they are real contumacies, not interpretative, apparent contumacies, not presumptive, that excommunicate a man in heaven. And much circumspection is required and (I am far from doubting it) exercised in those cases upon earth. For though every excommunication upon earth be not sealed in heaven, though it damn not the man, yet it dams[53] up that man's way by shutting him out of that church through which he must go to the other—which being so great a danger, let every man take heed of excommunicating himself. The impersuasible recusant[54] does so; the negligent libertine[55] does so; the fantastic Separatist[56] does so; the half-present man, he whose body is here and mind away, does so. And he whose body is but half here—his limbs are here upon a cushion, but his eyes, his cares are not here—does so. All these are self-excommunicators and keep themselves from hence. Only he enjoys that blessing, the

51. The contrast is between the church in heaven (triumphant) and the church on earth (militant). Donne is here interpreting "the power of the keys" (Matt. 16:19).

52. contumacy—perverse resistance to authority.

53. Donne's memorable wordplay ("damn . . . dams") is a brilliant example of how a poetic preacher may prompt theological reflection on the most serious of church controversies, making a point without belaboring it.

54. recusant—from about 1570 to 1791, the term that denoted a Roman Catholic who refused to attend services of the established church, thereby committing a statutory offense.

55. libertine—one who holds loose opinions about religion; a freethinker.

56. Separatist—in the seventeenth century, the term applied by members of the established church to the "Independents," who rejected all ecclesiastical

want whereof David deplores, that is here entirely, and is glad he is here, and glad to find this kind of service here that he does, and wishes no other.[57]

And so we have done with our first part: David's aspect, his present condition, and his danger of falling into spiritual miseries because his persecution and banishment amounted to an excommunication, to an excluding of him from the service of God in the church. And we pass, in our order proposed at first, to the second: his retrospect, the consideration what God had done for him before: "Because thou hast been my help."

PART II—REMEMBERING GOD'S PAST BENEFITS

Through this second part we shall pass by these three steps. First, that it behooves us in all our purposes and actions to propose to ourselves a copy to write by, a pattern to work by, a rule or an example to proceed by "Because it hath been thus heretofore," says David, "I will resolve upon this course for the future." And secondly, that the copy, the pattern, the precedent which we are to propose to ourselves is the observation of God's former ways and proceedings upon us. "Because God hath already gone this way, this way I will await his going still." And then, thirdly and lastly in this second part, the way that God had formerly gone with David, which was that he had been his help: "Because thou hast been my help."

Working by Pattern

First then, from the meanest artificer[58] through the wisest philosopher to God himself, all that is well done or wisely undertaken is undertaken and done according to preconceptions, foreimaginations, designs and patterns proposed to

authority outside the individual congregation.

57. Donne's words bespeak his conviction that there is no salvation for individuals apart from the church, and his further conviction that the established church (which he had entered as a convert from the Roman Church) was indeed a means of God's grace to the English nation.

58. meanest artificer—the most ordinary craftsman.

ourselves beforehand.[59] A carpenter builds not a house but that he first sets up a frame in his own mind what kind of house he will build. The little great philosopher Epictetus would undertake no action but he would first propose to himself what Socrates or Plato—what a wise man would do in that case, and according to that he would proceed. Of God himself, it is safely resolved in the school[60] that he never did any thing in any part of time of which he had not an eternal preconception, an eternal idea in himself before. Of which ideas—that is, preconceptions, predeterminations in God—St. Augustine pronounces, *Tanta vis in ideis constituitur:*[61] There is so much truth and so much power in these ideas as that without acknowledging them, no man can acknowledge God, for he does not allow God counsel and wisdom and deliberation in his actions but sets God on work before he have thought what he will do. And therefore he and others of the Fathers read that place (which we read otherwise), *Quod factum est, in ipso vita erat* (John 1:3–4).[62] That is, in all their expositions, whatsoever is made in time was alive in God before it was made, that is, in that eternal idea and pattern which was in him. So also do diverse of those Fathers read those words to the Hebrews (which we read, "The things that are seen are not made of things that do appear"): *Ex invisibilibus visibilia facta sunt,* "Things formerly invisible were made visible" (Heb. 11:3).[63] That is, we see them not till now, till they are made, but they had an invisible being in that idea, in that pre-notion, in that purpose of God before, forever before. Of all things in heaven and earth but of himself God had an idea, a pattern in himself, before he made it.

And therefore let him be our pattern for that, to work after patterns. To propose to our-

59. In this section Donne explores at length a key concept of Christian Neoplatonism, the preexistence of ideal forms. The discussion is tangentially related to a central theme of the sermon, namely, the necessity of participating in established patterns of faith and worship. Although he left the Roman Church to join the reformed Church of England, Donne considered himself a member of the "catholic church." He was firmly convinced of the indispensability of following the church's traditional teachings and adhering to a set liturgy and pattern for prayer; this last is one reason why Donne so often preached on the psalms.

60. Donne refers here to the medieval tradition of scholastic Christian philosophy.

61. Augustine, *De diversis quaestionibus* 1.46 (PL 40:29).

62. According to the Vulgate reading, the two phrases belong to different verses:

[3]. . . et sine ipso factum est nihil, *quod factum est* [. . . and without him nothing was made, *which was made*]. [4]In ipso vita erat . . . [*In him was life*].

The patristic reading that Donne cites connects the phrases in a single idea: "That which was made, in him it was (a) life." Augustine, *In Joannis Evangelium* 1.16 (PL 35:1387).

63. As is his custom, Donne cites the text in the 1611 Authorized (King James) Version. The NRSV renders the passage somewhat differently from either translational option Donne cites: "Now faith is the assurance of things hoped for, the conviction of things not seen . . . . By faith we understand that the worlds were prepared by the word of God, so that *what is seen was made from things that are not visible*" (vv. 1, 3).

selves rules and examples for all our actions—
and the more, the more immediately, the more
directly our actions concern the service of God.
If I ask God by what idea he made me, God produces his *Faciamus hominem ad imaginem . . .
nostrum* [Gen. 1:26],[64] that there was a concurrence of the whole Trinity to make me (in
Adam) according to that image which they
were, and according to that idea which they
had predetermined. If I pretend[65] to serve God
and he ask me for my idea how I mean to serve
him, shall I be able to produce none? If he ask
me an idea of my religion and my opinions,
shall I not be able to say, "It is that which thy
Word and thy catholic church hath imprinted in
me"? If he ask me an idea of my prayers, shall I
not be able to say, "It is that which my particular necessities, that which the form prescribed
by thy Son, that which the care and piety of the
church in conceiving fit prayers hath imprinted
in me"? If he ask me an idea of my sermons,
shall I not be able to say, "It is that which the
analogy of faith, the edification of the congregation, the zeal of thy work, the meditations of
my heart have imprinted in me"? But if I come
to pray or to preach without this kind of idea, if
I come to extemporal prayer and extemporal
preaching, I shall come to an extemporal faith
and extemporal religion. And then I must look
for an extemporal heaven, a heaven to be
made for me. For to that heaven which belongs
to the catholic church I shall never come except
I go by the way of the catholic church: by former ideas, former examples, former patterns,
to believe according to ancient beliefs, to pray
according to ancient forms, to preach according to former meditations. God does nothing,
man does nothing well—without these ideas,
these retrospects, this recourse to preconceptions, pre-deliberations.

64. "Let us make man according to our image." Donne
slightly abbreviates the Vulgate
reading, *Faciamus hominem ad
imaginem et similitudinem nostrum.*

65. Donne uses the word
"pretend" in a positive sense: "If
I aspire . . ."

God's Way in the Past

Something then I must propose to myself, to be the rule and the reason of my present and future actions, which was our first branch in this second part. And then the second is that I can propose nothing more availably than the contemplation of the history of God's former proceeding with me, which is David's way here. Because this was God's way before, I will look for God in this way still. That language in which God spoke to man, the Hebrew, hath no present tense.[66] They form not their verbs as our Western languages do, in the present: "I hear," or "I see," or "I read." But they begin at that which is past: "I have seen, and heard, and read." God carries us in his language, in his speaking, upon that which is past, upon that which he hath done already. I cannot have better security for present nor future than God's former mercies exhibited to me. *Quis . . . non gaudeat*, says St. Augustine, "Who does not triumph with joy," when he considers what God hath done? *Quis non et ea quae nondum venerunt ventura sperat, propter illa quae iam tanta impleta sunt?*[67] Who can doubt of the performance of all, that sees the greatest part of a prophecy performed? If I have found that true that God hath said of the person of Antichrist, why should I doubt of that which he says of the ruin of Antichrist? *Credamus modicum quod restat*,[68] says the same Father. It is much that we have seen done, and it is but little that God hath reserved to our faith, to believe that it shall be done.[69]

There is no state, no church, no man that hath not this tie upon God, that hath not God in these bands: that God by having done much for them already hath bound himself to do more.[70] Men proceed in their former ways sometimes lest they should confess an error and acknowledge that they had been in a wrong

66. Donne studied Hebrew as a student at Oxford and again when he began to consider Holy Orders, in 1613. He seems to have had a much greater interest in Hebrew than in Greek and makes frequent reference to it in his sermons. See Potter and Simpson, *Sermons of John Donne*, 10:306–12.

67. "Who does not hope that those things too that have not yet come will come, because of those things so many of which have already been fulfilled?" Augustine, *Enarrationes in Psalmos* 42.1 (PL 36:748).

68. "Let us hold in faith the small amount that remains." Ibid.

69. Donne places high value on history and memory—and especially the corporate history and memory preserved in Scripture—as essential to faith: "The art of salvation is but the art of memory." Donne, Sermon on Psalm 38:3 (Potter and Simpson, *Sermons of John Donne*, 2:73).

70. The fourteenth-century mystic Catherine of Siena chooses a similar image to

way. God is obnoxious to[71] no error, and therefore he does still as he did before. Every one of
you can say now to God: "Lord, thou brought-
est me hither; therefore enable me to hear.
Lord, thou doest that; therefore make me
understand. And that; therefore let me believe.
And that too; therefore strengthen me to the
practice. And all that; therefore continue me to
a perseverance." Carry it up to the first sense
and apprehension that ever thou hadst of God's
working upon thee, either in thyself when thou
camest first to the use of reason,
or in others in thy behalf in thy baptism. Yet
when thou thinkest thou art at the first, God
had done something for thee before all that.
Before that, he had elected thee in that election which St. Augustine speaks of, *Habet elec-
tos quos creaturus est eligendos*, "God hath
elected certain men whom he intends to create
that he may elect them"[72]—that is, that he may
declare his election upon them. God had thee
before he made thee. He loved thee first and
then created thee, that thou loving him, he
might continue his love to thee. The surest way,
and the nearest way to lay hold upon God is the
consideration of that which he had done
already. So David does. And that which he takes
knowledge of, in particular, in God's former
proceedings towards him, is "Because God had
been his help," which is our last branch in this
part: "Because thou hast been my help."

Because Thou Hast Been My Help

From this one word, that God hath been *my
help*, I make account that we have both these
notions: first, that God hath not left me to
myself. He hath come to my succor; he hath
helped me. And then, that God hath not left
out myself. He hath been my help, but he hath
left something for me to do with him and by his

express a bold theology of
prayer akin to Donne's:
"Blessed, O most generous
Father, be the chain you have
given us with which we can tie
the hands of your justice, the
chain of your servants' humble
faithful prayer ablaze with
desire, for you have promised to
use them to be merciful to the
world." *The Prayers of Catherine
of Siena*, ed. Suzanne Noffke,
OP (Ramsey, N.J.: Paulist Press,
1983), 64. Both Catherine and
Donne probably took from the
psalms the conviction that
God's past faithfulness, evidenced above all in delivering
the ancestors and entering into
covenant with them, "con-
strains" God to continue such
saving action (e.g., Ps. 22:5 [4
Eng.]).
71. obnoxious to—suscepti-
ble to.

72. Augustine, *Sermones* 26.4
(PL 38:173).

help. My security for the future, in this consideration of that which is past, lies not only in this—that God hath delivered me—but in this also: that he hath delivered me by way of a help, and help always presumes an endeavor and cooperation in him that is helped. God did not elect me as a helper, nor create me, nor redeem me, nor convert me by way of helping me. For he alone did all, and he had no use at all of me. God infuses his first grace, the first way, merely as a giver, entirely all himself, but his subsequent graces, as a helper. Therefore we call them "auxiliant graces," helping graces, and we always receive them when we endeavor to make use of his former grace.[73] "Lord, I believe," says the man in the Gospel to Christ; "Help mine unbelief!" (Mark 9:24). If there had not been unbelief, weakness, unperfectness in that faith, there had needed no help. But if there had not been a belief, a faith, it had not been capable of help and assistance, but it must have been an entire act, without any concurrence on the man's part.

So that if I have truly the testimony of a rectified conscience that God hath helped me, it is in both respects: first, that he hath never forsaken me; and then, that he hath never suffered me to forsake myself. He hath blessed me with that grace, that I trust in no help but his, and with this grace too, that I cannot look for his help except I help myself also. God did not "help" heaven and earth to proceed out of nothing in the Creation, for they had no possibility of any disposition towards it—for they had no being. But God did "help" the earth to produce grasses and herbs. For, for that, God had infused a seminal disposition into the earth, which, for all that, it could not have perfected without his farther help. As in the making of woman, there is the very word of our

73. Donne's conviction that God supplies us with *helping* graces marks his theological position as Arminian (named after the Dutch theologian Jacobus Arminius [1560–1609]). Although Donne consults Calvin and sometimes cites him approvingly, he does not adopt a strict Calvinist view that humankind is redeemed exclusively through God's *irresistible* grace—which, in our depravity, we would resist if we could, and with which we are incapable of cooperating.

text, *gnazar*,[74] God made him a "helper," one that was to do much for him, but not without him. So that then, if I will make God's former working upon me an argument of his future gracious purposes, as I must acknowledge that God hath done much for me, so I must find that I have done what I could by the benefit of that grace with him: for God promises to be but a helper. "Lord, open thou my lips" (Ps. 51:15), says David. That is God's work entirely. And then, "my mouth"—"My mouth shall show forth thy praise." There enters David into the work with God. And then says God to him: *Dilata os tuum*, "Open thy mouth . . ." (it is now made "thy" mouth, and therefore do thou open it) ". . . and I will fill it" (Ps. 81:10). All inchoations and consummations, beginnings and perfectings, are of God, of God alone. But in the way there is a concurrence on our part, by a successive continuation of God's grace, in which God proceeds as a helper—and I put him to more than that, if I do nothing. But if I pray for his help, and apprehend and husband his graces well when they come, then he is truly, properly my helper. And upon that security, that testimony of a rectified conscience, I can proceed to David's confidence for the future: "Because thou hast been my help, therefore in the shadow of thy wings will I rejoice"—which is our third and last general part.

PART III—ASSURANCE FOR THE FUTURE

In this last part, which is (after David's aspect and consideration of his present condition, which was, in the effect, an exclusion from God's temple, and his retrospect, his consideration of God's former mercies to him, that he had been his help) his prospect, his confidence for the future, we shall stay a little upon these

74. This is a rough transliteration of the Hebrew word עֵזֶר (*ʿezer*), "help" (Gen. 2:18, 20). The positive comparison between God and Eve is noteworthy, as premodern theologians often placed disproportionate blame on Eve for the original disobedience. The comparison is in fact exegetically sound, as apart from Eve the word is most memorably and frequently applied to God (Pss. 33:20; 70:6 [5 Eng.]; 146:5, etc.). Donne's high regard for women, and especially his own wife, Ann (whom he credited with nurturing his own mature faith), may further inform this comparison.

two steps: first, that that which he promises himself is not an immunity from all powerful enemies, nor a sword of revenge upon those enemies. It is not that he shall have no adversary, nor that that adversary shall be able to do him no harm, but that he should have a refreshing, a respiration, *in velamento alarum*, "under the shadow of God's wings." And then (in the second place), that this way which God shall be pleased to take, this manner, this measure of refreshing which God shall vouchsafe to afford—though it amount not to a full deliverance—must produce a joy, a rejoicing in us. We must not only not decline to a murmuring that we have no more, no, nor rest upon a patience for that which remains, but we must ascend to a holy joy as if all were done and accomplished: "In the shadow of thy wings will I rejoice."

The Shadow of God's Wings

First then (lest any man in his dejection of spirit or of fortune should stray into a jealousy or suspicion of God's power to deliver him), as God hath spangled the firmament with stars, so hath he his Scriptures with names and metaphors and denotations of power.[75] Sometimes he shines out in the name of a sword, and of a target, and of a wall, and of a tower, and of a rock, and of a hill. And sometimes in that glorious and manifold constellation of all together, *Dominus exercituum*, "the Lord of Hosts." God as God is never represented to us with defensive arms; he needs them not. When the poets present their great heroes and their worthies, they always insist upon their arms. They spend much of their invention upon the description of their arms, both because the greatest valor and strength needs arms (Goliath himself was armed) and because to expose oneself to danger unarmed is not valor but rashness. But God is invulnerable

75. Donne's own consummate skill as a poet and writer is reflected in this discussion of the metaphors of Scripture and how they accurately portray complex theological truths. Donne's subtle reading of the metaphor of wings as denoting divine power but not full deliverance bespeaks a profound understanding of the assurances of Scripture, which take full account of the persistent difficulties experienced by the faithful in this life. The modesty of Donne's application of the metaphor argues for a modification of John Carey's claim that Donne's poems—and even more, his sermons—represent "the most enduring exhibition of the will to power the English Renaissance produced." John Carey, *John Donne: Life, Mind, and Art* (London: Faber & Faber, 1990), 108.

in himself and is never represented armed; you find no shirts of mail, no helmets, no cuirasses[76] in God's armory. In that one place of Isaiah where it may seem to be otherwise, where God is said to have "put on righteousness as a breast-plate, and a helmet of salvation upon his head" (Isa. 59:17)—in that prophecy God is Christ and is therefore in that place called "the Redeemer" [v. 20]. Christ needed defensive arms; God does not. God's Word does, his Scriptures do, and therefore St. Jerome hath "armed" them and set before every book his *Prologum galeatum,*[77] that prologue that arms and defends every book from calumny. But though God need not nor receive not defensive arms for himself, yet God is to us a helmet, a breastplate, a strong tower, a rock—everything that may give us assurance and defense. And as often as he will, he can refresh that proclamation, *Nolite tangere christos meos* (Ps. 105:15),[78] our enemies shall not so much as touch us.

But here, by occasion of his metaphor in this text—*sub umbra alarum,* "in the shadow of thy wings"—we do not so much consider an absolute immunity, that we shall not be touched, as a refreshing and consolation when we are touched, though we be pinched and wounded. The names of God which are most frequent in the Scriptures are these three: *Elohim,* and *Adonai,* and *Jehovah.* And to assure us of his power to deliver us, two of these three are names of power. *Elohim* is *Deus fortis,* the mighty, the powerful God. And (which deserves a particular consideration) *Elohim* is a plural name; it is not *Deus fortis* but *Dii fortes,* powerful Gods. God is all kind of gods: all kinds which either idolaters and Gentiles can imagine (as riches, or justice, or wisdom, or valor, or such), and all kinds which God himself hath called "gods" (as princes, and magistrates, and prelates, and all

76. cuirass—a piece of armor consisting of a breastplate and a backplate, originally of leather.

77. *Prologum galeatum*—literally, a helmeted prologue. Jerome's *Prologus galeatus,* a brief overview and defense of Jerome's approach to the Old Testament canon and its translation from the Hebrew, is named for a statement in its final paragraph: "This preface to the Scriptures may serve as a 'helmeted' introduction to all the books which we turn from Hebrew into Latin, so that we may be assured that what is not found in our list must be placed amongst the Apocryphal writings." Although written as a prologue to the books of Samuel and Kings, in some editions of the Latin Vulgate it was placed (together with Jerome's other prologues) at the front of the Bible. See Mueller, *Donne's Prebend Sermons,* 238; Robert Weber, preface to *Biblia Sacra: Juxta Vulgatam Versionem,* 2 vols. (Stuttgart: Württembergische Bibelanstalt, 1969), 1:xxi. For the English translation, see *NPNF*[2] 6:489–90.
78. "Do not touch my anointed [*christos*; Hebrew, מְשִׁיחָי (*mᵉshîhai*)]."

that assist and help one another). God is *Elohim:* all these gods, and all these in their height and best of their power. For *Elohim* is *Dii fortes,* "gods" in the plural, and those plural gods in their exaltation.

The second name of God is a name of power too: *Adonai.* For *Adonai* is *Dominus,* the Lord, such a Lord as is Lord and proprietary of all his creatures, and all creatures are his creatures. And then, *Dominium est potestas tum utendi, tum abutendi,* says the law: to be absolute lord of any thing gives that lord a power to do what he will with that thing.[79] God, as he is *Adonai,* the Lord, may give and take [Job 1:21], quicken and kill [1 Sam. 2:6], build and throw down [Jer. 1:10; Eccl. 3:3; 2 Cor. 13:10], where and whom he will. So then two of God's three names are names of absolute power, to imprint and re-imprint an assurance in us that he can absolutely deliver us and fully revenge us, if he will. But then his third name—and that name which he chooses to himself, and in the signification of which name he employs Moses for the relief of his people under Pharaoh—that name *Jehovah* is not a name of power but only of essence, of being, of subsistence. And yet in the virtue of that name, God relieved his people.[80] And if, in my afflictions, God vouchsafe to visit me in that name, to preserve me in my being—in my subsistence in him that I be not shaked out of him, disinherited in him, excommunicate from him, divested of him, annihilated towards him—let him at his good pleasure reserve his *Elohim* and his *Adonai,* the exercises and declarations of his mighty power, to those great public causes that more concern his glory than any thing that can befall me. But if he impart his *Jehovah,* enlarge himself so far towards me as that I may "live and move and have my being in him" [Acts 17:28], though I be not instantly delivered nor mine

79. Donne draws upon his early legal training (at Lincoln's Inn, London) to cite a definition in secular law: "Lordship is the power at one time to use, at another time to waste."

80. This is of course the divine name revealed to Moses at the burning bush (Exod. 3:13–18), when he is commissioned to confront Pharaoh and speak to the Israelites in the name of YHWH (for Donne, "Jehovah").

enemies absolutely destroyed, yet this is as much as I should promise myself; this is as much as the Holy Ghost intends in this metaphor. *Sub umbra alarum*, "under the shadow of thy wings"—that is a refreshing, a respiration, a conservation, a consolation in all afflictions that are inflicted upon me.

Yet is not this metaphor of *wings* without a denotation of power. As no act of God's, though it seems to imply but spiritual comfort, is without a denotation of power—for it is the power of God that comforts me; to overcome that sadness of soul and that dejection of spirit which the Adversary by temporal afflictions would induce upon me is an act of his power[81] —so this metaphor, the shadow of his wings (which in this place expresses no more than consolation and refreshing in misery, and not a powerful deliverance out of it) is so often in the Scriptures made a denotation of power too as that we can doubt of no act of power if we have this shadow of his wings. For in this metaphor of wings doth the Holy Ghost express the maritime power, the power of some nations at sea, in navies: "Woe to the land shadowing with wings" (Isa. 18:1)—that is, that hovers over the world and intimidates it with her sails and ships. In this metaphor doth God remember[82] his people of his powerful deliverance of them: "You have seen what I did unto the Egyptians, and how I bare you on eagles' wings, and brought you to myself" (Exod. 19:4). In this metaphor doth God threaten his and their enemies, what he can do: "The noise of the wings of his cherubims are as the noise of great waters, and of an army" (Ezek. 1:24). So also, what he will do: "He shall spread his wings over Bozrah, and at that day shall the hearts of the mighty men of Edom be as the heart of a woman in her pangs" (Jer. 49:22). So that if I

81. In this aside, Donne speaks from his own experience of depression here, a condition to which he shows great pastoral sensitivity (see the sermon's final section, "Joy," below).

82. remember—remind.

have the shadow of his wings, I have the earnest of the power of them too. If I have refreshing and respiration from them, I am able to say (as those three confessors[83] did to Nebuchadnezzar): "My God is able to deliver me," I am sure he hath power; "And my God will deliver me," when it conduces to his glory, I know he will; "But, if he do not, be it known unto thee, O King, we will not serve thy gods" (Dan. 3:17[–18]). Be it known unto thee, O Satan, how long soever God defer my deliverance, I will not seek false comforts, the miserable comforts of this world. I will not, for I need not; for I can subsist under this shadow of these wings, though I have no more.

The mercy seat itself was covered with the cherubim's wings (Exod. 25:20), and who would have more than mercy? And a mercy seat—that is, established, resident mercy, permanent and perpetual mercy, present and familiar mercy; a mercy seat. Our Savior Christ intends as much as would have served their turn if they had laid hold upon it when he says that he "would have gathered Jerusalem, as a hen gathers her chickens under her wings" (Matt. 23:37). And though the other prophets do (as ye have heard) mingle the signification of power and actual deliverance in this metaphor of wings, yet our prophet, whom we have now in special consideration, David, never doth so.[84] But in every place where he uses this metaphor of wings (which are in five or six several psalms), still he rests and determines in that sense which is his meaning here: that though God does not actually deliver us, nor actually destroy our enemies, yet if he refresh us in the shadow of his wings, if he maintain our subsistence (which is a religious constancy) in him, this should not only establish our patience (for that is but half the work), but it should also produce a joy and rise to an exul-

83. Donne probably means "confessors" in the technical sense, i.e., those who have been tortured (but not killed) for the sake of God's name.

84. Like all premodern Christians, Donne considered "David" (the psalmist) a prophet of Christ. His keen awareness of the different uses of the metaphor of wings in the Psalms and in the Prophets is a noteworthy example of premodern scholarship that is fully critical.

tation, which is our last circumstance: "Therefore in the shadow of thy wings, I will rejoice."

Joy

I would always raise your hearts and dilate your
hearts to a holy joy, to a joy in the Holy Ghost.
There may be a just fear that men do not grieve
enough for their sins, but there may be a just
jealousy[85] and suspicion too that they may fall
into inordinate grief and diffidence of God's
mercy. And God hath reserved us to such times
as (being the later times) give us even the dregs
and lees of misery to drink. For God hath not
only let loose into the world a new spiritual disease, which is an equality and an indifferency,
which religion our children or our servants or
our companions profess. (I would not keep
company with a man that thought me a knave
or a traitor; with him that thought I loved not
my Prince or were a faithless man, not to be
believed, I would not associate myself. And yet
I will make him my bosom companion that
thinks I do not love God, that thinks I cannot be
saved.) But God hath accompanied and complicated almost all our bodily diseases of these
times with an extraordinary sadness, a predom-
inant melancholy, a faintness of heart, a cheer-
lessness, a joylessness of spirit, and therefore I
return often to this endeavor of raising your
hearts, dilating your hearts with a holy joy, joy
in the Holy Ghost, for "under the shadow of his
wings," you may, you should, "rejoice."

If you look upon this world in a map, you
find two hemispheres, two half-worlds. If you
crush heaven into a map, you may find two
hemispheres too, two half-heavens: half will be
joy and half will be glory. For in these two, the
joy of heaven and the glory of heaven, is all
heaven often represented unto us. And as of
those two hemispheres of the world, the first

85. "Jealousy" in this sense
denotes doubt or anxiety.

hath been known long before, but the other (that of America, which is the richer in treasure) God reserved for later discoveries, so though he reserve that hemisphere of heaven, which is the glory thereof, to the resurrection, yet the other hemisphere, the joy of heaven, God opens to our discovery and delivers for our habitation even whilst we dwell in this world. As God hath cast upon the unrepentant sinner two deaths, a temporal and a spiritual death, so hath he breathed into us two lives. For so, as the word for "death" is doubled, *Morte morieris*, "Thou shalt die the death" (Gen. 2:17), so is the word for "life" expressed in the plural: *Chaiim, vitarum*, "God breathed into his nostrils the breath of lives" [Gen. 2:7]—of diverse lives.[86] Though our natural life were no life but rather a continual dying, yet we have two lives besides that: an eternal life reserved for heaven, but yet a heavenly life too, a spiritual life even in this world. And as God doth thus inflict two deaths and infuse two lives, so doth he also pass two judgments upon man, or rather repeats the same judgment twice. For that which Christ shall say to thy soul then at the last judgment, "Enter into thy master's joy" (Matt. 25:23 GB), he says to thy conscience now, "Enter into thy master's joy." The everlastingness of the joy is the blessedness of the next life, but the entering, the inchoation, is afforded here. For that which Christ shall say then to us, *Venite benedicti*, "Come ye blessed" (v. 34), are words intended to persons that are coming, that are upon the way, though not at home. Here in this world he bids us "Come"; there in the next he shall bid us "Welcome." The angels of heaven have joy in thy conversion (Luke 15:10), and canst thou be without that joy in thyself? If thou desire revenge upon thine enemies—as they are God's enemies—that God would be pleased to remove and root out all

86. Donne's "grammatical exegesis" here is fanciful but not idiosyncratic. His wordplay on Hebrew syntax and morphology is in the style of rabbinic exegesis, with which he had some familiarity. See Potter and Simpson, *Sermons of John Donne*, 10:307.

such as oppose him,[87] that affection appertains to glory. Let that alone till thou come to the hemisphere of glory. There join with those martyrs under the altar—*Usquequo Domine*, "How long, O Lord, . . . dost thou defer judgment?" (Rev. 6:10)—and thou shalt have thine answer there for that.

Whilst thou art here, here join with David and the other saints of God in that holy increpation[88] of a dangerous sadness, "Why art thou cast down, O my soul? Why art thou disquieted in me?" (Ps. 42:5). That soul that is dissected and anatomized to God in a sincere confession, washed in the tears of true contrition, embalmed in the blood of reconciliation, the blood of Christ Jesus, can assign no reason, can give no just answer to that interrogatory, "Why art thou cast down, O my soul? Why art thou disquieted in me?" No man is so little as that he can be lost under these wings, no man so great as that they cannot reach to him. *Semper ille major est, quantumcumque creverimus.*[89] To what temporal, to what spiritual greatnesses soever we grow, still pray we him to shadow us under his wings, for the poor need those wings against oppression and the rich against envy.

The Holy Ghost, who is a dove, shadowed the whole world under his wings. *Incubabat aquis*, "he hovered over the waters" [Gen. 1:2]; he sat upon the waters, and he hatched all that was produced, and all that was produced so was good. Be thou a mother where the Holy Ghost would be a mother. Conceive by him,[90] and be content that he produce joy in thy heart here. First think that as a man must have some land or else he cannot be in wardship, so a man must have some of the love of God or else he could not fall under God's correction.[91] God would not give him his physic,[92] God would not study his cure if he cared not for him. And then

87. Although Donne is preaching on only one verse of Psalm 63, this comment indicates that he takes account of the whole, which concludes with an imprecation on the psalmist's enemies (vv. 10–12 [9–11 Eng.]).

88. increpation—rebuke.

89. "Always he is greater, however great we may grow." Augustine, *Enarrationes in Psalmos* 42.16 (PL 36:758).

90. With this daring metaphor, Donne is calling his audience to participate in a new "incarnation."
91. Donne's metaphor of wardship (whereby both an underage heir and the inherited land were placed in the care of a guardian) implies that the love of God is a kind of inheritance or spiritual property, but one that we are probably not yet mature enough to handle well.
92. physic—medicine.

think also that if God afford thee the shadow of his wings, that is, consolation, respiration, refreshing—though not a present and plenary deliverance—in thy afflictions, not to thank God is a murmuring, and not to rejoice in God's ways is an unthankfulness.

Howling is the noise of hell; singing the voice of heaven. Sadness the damp of hell; rejoicing the serenity of heaven. And he that hath not this joy here lacks one of the best pieces of his evidence for the joys of heaven, and hath neglected or refused that earnest by which God uses to bind his bargain, that true joy in this world shall flow into the joy of heaven as a river flows into the sea. This joy shall not be put out in death and a new joy kindled in me in heaven. But as my soul, as soon as it is out of my body, is in heaven, and does not stay[93] for the possession of heaven nor for the fruition of the sight of God till it be ascended through air, and fire, and moon, and sun, and planets, and firmament to that place which we conceive to be heaven, but without the thousandth part of a minute's stop, as soon as it issues, is in a glorious light, which is heaven . . . (For all the way to heaven is heaven. And as those angels which came from heaven hither bring heaven with them and are in heaven here, so that soul that goes to heaven meets heaven here. And as those angels do not divest heaven by coming, so these souls invest heaven in their going.) As my soul shall not go towards heaven but go by heaven to heaven, to the heaven of heavens, so the true joy of a good soul in this world is the very joy of heaven. And we go thither, not that being without joy we might have joy infused into us, but that, as Christ says, "our joy might be full" (John 16:24), perfected, sealed with an everlastingness. For as he promises that "no man shall take our joy

93. stay—wait.

from us" (v. 22 GB), so neither shall Death itself take it away, nor so much as interrupt it or discontinue it. But as in the face of Death, when he lays hold upon me, and in the face of the devil, when he attempts me, I shall see the face of God (for everything shall be a glass,[94] to reflect God upon me), so in the agonies of death, in the anguish of that dissolution, in the sorrows of that valediction, in the irreversibleness of that transmigration, I shall have a joy which shall no more evaporate than my soul shall evaporate—a joy that shall pass up and put on a more glorious garment above and be joy super-invested[95] in glory. Amen.

94. glass—looking glass.

95. "Super-invested" is a typical example of Donne's tendency to coin new words in the sermons, and, as John Carey observes, "'super-' is an especially appealing prefix, since it cancels and surpasses any chosen word even before that word has been written down. It reinforces the effort to make language reach beyond language which is constantly discernible in Donne's religious paroxysms." Carey cites multiple examples of such compounds, most of which do not make strict logical sense: super-canonization, super-catholic, super-dying, super-edifications, super-Reformation, super-universal, super-miraculous, super-exaltation, super-infinite. Carey, *John Donne*, 113.

CHAPTER 3

An Abundance of Meaning

New Testament scholar Leander Keck cites a comment made by a student who had been a lay preacher before beginning formal theological study: "I could preach a whole lot better before I took your [New Testament interpretation] course."[1] I think most of us who teach Bible harbor a guilty suspicion that someone in the class is always thinking that—and not entirely without justification. For even if this student remembers his early preaching as better than it was, his comment nonetheless points to a real and discomforting fact, namely, that the connection between writing an exegesis paper and writing a sermon is so often hard to perceive, despite the best intentions of those who teach and write with the church's needs in mind.

I have yet to resolve this problem in my own teaching, especially at the introductory level, or even to see clearly its full dimensions. However, it seems to me that this is at its heart: critical biblical study is historical, and necessarily so, but today it is historical in too narrow a sense. We who teach Bible focus largely on the historical, social, and political circumstances that may underlie the composition and redaction of a given text, supposing that these provide the information we need to identify its meaning. And generally, the implication is that the text means only one thing: what it meant in its ancient context—the scorn of postmodernism notwithstanding.[2]

---

1. Leander E. Keck, "The Premodern Bible in the Postmodern World," *Interpretation* 50 (1996): 139.
2. Drawing on premodern hermeneutics, David Steinmetz has written a now-classic critique of the modern assumption of a single meaning, identified with the author's intention. See "The Superiority of Pre-Critical Exegesis," in *The Theological Interpretation of Scripture*, ed. Stephen Fowl (Cambridge, Mass.:

That notion of a single correct meaning is the source of great anxiety to first-year divinity school students writing exegesis papers: What if I can't figure it out? What if I get it wrong? But more telling of the problem for preachers is the fact that the idea hangs on, and once those students graduate and become pastors, the notion that meaning is a fixed historical datum is still a source of anxiety. For now they see themselves as something like homiletical archaeologists, responsible for unearthing that artifact, "the meaning," and interpreting it for an audience that does not understand its (presumed) original context. Moreover—unlike real archaeologists—they must persuade their hearers that that antique datum is somehow of immediate and personal interest. They must help them find for it a new context of meaning in their own lives, in the contemporary world.

Accomplishing that recontextualization is a difficult imaginative task. So it is not surprising that the category of imagination now plays a large role in homiletical discussion, even if it remains difficult to integrate that discussion with historically oriented biblical studies. Aware that there is a problem, some biblical scholars decide that historical study is itself the problem, so they turn to forms of literary and ideological criticism that make light use of history and focus instead on current reception and use of the text. Such studies often celebrate the adventure of reading and the reader's use of imagination to construct meaning and "fashion the world through language,"[3] notions that might be expected to appeal to contemporary preachers. Yet my experience is that students are frequently disappointed in "literary readings" of biblical texts, because they tend to gloss over the theological concerns that the students themselves see reflected there. To the extent that scholars ignore what was in most cases the chief interest of the biblical author or redactor, they produce readings that are historically implausible and, moreover, don't preach.

Blackwell, 1997), 26–38. More recently, Daniel Hardy, observing that most modern reading strategies "have been predicated on harsh ways of reducing the enormous density of meaning in the Scriptures," has argued that benefiting from this density, in part by means of arguments about meaning, is the aim of reading Scripture in community. Daniel Hardy, "Reason, Wisdom, and the Interpretation of Scripture," in *Reading Texts, Seeking Wisdom: Scripture and Theology*, ed. David Ford and Graham Stanton (Grand Rapids: Eerdmans, 2004), 88.

3. The phrase is taken from David Gunn and Danna Nolan Fewell's discussion of the "rhetorical" view of human nature and truth itself: "The 'rhetorical' human fashions the world through language, manipulating reality rather than discovering it, since reality is that which is construed as reality rather than some objective essence. . . . This world is a carnivalesque one of exuberance and possibility, of enthusiasm and metaphor, of religion, magic, and verbal incantation, where truth is 'an artifact whose fundamental design we often have to alter.'" David M. Gunn and Danna Nolan Fewell, *Narrative in the Hebrew Bible* (Oxford: Oxford University Press, 1993), 10, quoting Richard Rorty, *The Consequences of Pragmatism* (Minneapolis: University of Minnesota Press, 1982), 92.

In order to be helpful for preaching, biblical studies need to take history seriously, while at the same time taking account of the fact that preaching is not an antiquarian or archaeological endeavor. No one would try to preach the *Enuma Elish*. We can preach from the Bible only because it is not an excavated text but a traditional one, one that has from the time of its composition been passed from hand to hand and mouth to ear, from generation to generation in Israel and the church. And so my proposal is that preaching would benefit from critical biblical studies that reflect a more inclusive view of a text's history, a view that takes into account not only its supposed original meaning but also the abundance of meaning that has been found in the text through the centuries by Jews and Christians. We can interpret the Bible for the Christian life—and interpret it accurately, skillfully, even beautifully—only because others have consistently done so before us. Because the space between us and the original *Sitz im Leben* of a given text is not empty, an approach to biblical study that is fully critical and therefore most helpful to preachers must include awareness of the riches that fill that space.

To sum up my proposal in a single phrase, I suggest that *interpretation of the Bible for the church's life is a traditional art.* I take that notion from Seyyed Hossein Nasr's argument, presented in his 1981 Gifford Lectures, for a renewed appreciation of traditional wisdom, or "sacred knowledge," among all three of the Abrahamic traditions. Nasr argues further that significant achievements in the applied arts—for instance, the architecture and engineering that enabled construction of medieval cathedrals in Europe and, at approximately the same time, magnificent mosques in Asia and Egypt—are an essential expression of the intellectual vitality of a culture that values knowledge of the sacred.[4] Artists working in a sacred tradition do not see themselves as independent geniuses, no matter how brilliant their individual talent. Rather than engaging in self-expression, they are putting their skill at the service of a vision that exceeds their own in both scope and duration. They work by pattern, using established forms and symbols. Their genius is to work with old forms in ways that realize new possibilities, enriching and reinvigorating the tradition without breaking it. Occasionally some expression of the expansive vision carried by the tradition will be brought to the acme of perfection; one thinks of the rose window at Chartres, for instance, or many parts of Scripture itself. Yet even those works of consummate genius are not

---

4. Seyyed Hossein Nasr, *Knowledge and the Sacred*, Gifford Lectures, 1981 (New York: Crossroad, 1981), 258.

highly individualized "pieces of art." Rather, they are identifiably products and expressions of skilled work practices, aesthetic judgments, and theological understandings shared by multiple generations and communities. Although Nasr confines his discussion to the tangible crafts, the work of artisans, I believe that much of what he says about the practice of traditional arts applies also to biblical interpretation done in the context of a community of living faith—and, by extension, to preaching.

Most preachers I know find their job difficult, and it is. No practice of an art is easy, but my aim here is to offer practical encouragement and help. I hope to show that practicing interpretation and preaching as traditional arts has distinct advantages, with respect to both what we see in the biblical text and how we understand our own role as interpreters. The chief of those advantages is that the text appears more wondrous when viewed through the lens of the Christian tradition of theology and liturgy. The poet who wrote Psalm 119 was himself deeply engaged in such a tradition of study and worship, and it disposed him to be awestruck by the divine Word: גַּל־עֵינַי וְאַבִּיטָה נִפְלָאוֹת מִתּוֹרָתֶךָ (gal-ʿênai vᵉʾabbîtah niflāʾôt mittôratekha), "Open my eyes that I may look upon wonders from your Torah" (v. 18). With eyes and mind enriched by gifts of insight received from our predecessors, we begin to see, not a single fixed meaning, but the abundance of potential meanings that premodern interpreters knew to reside in the biblical text. The Bible is inexhaustibly rich in meaning, and that is the best reason to preach from it week after week. It is also the reason to read it "intensively,"[5] dwelling on its particular words, as did ancient and medieval Jews and Christians. הֲפוֹךְ בַּהּ וַהֲפוֹךְ בַּהּ (hafôkh bah vahafôkh bah), the early rabbis say: "*Keep turning it over and over, for everything is in it—and through it, you will get vision.*"[6] If most contemporary readers find a richly repetitive poem like Psalm 119 merely tedious, that is some measure of how far we are from the kind of awe that enables one to gaze tirelessly at the divine Word, wonderstruck as a new parent gazing at her child.

Yet the conviction that there is always more meaning to be found even—and perhaps especially—in a familiar text is not wholly a pious

---

5. I take the phrase from Russell Reno's helpful description of the style of patristic biblical commentary: "Unlike figural interpretation, . . . intensive reading focuses on the semantic plenitude of particular scriptural signs or episodes. Patristic commentary on the Gospel of John is paradigmatic. Origen, for example, gathers up many meanings of *logos*, and he does so not to sift through them and settle upon a single and univocal meaning, but in order to arrange the many meanings around the christological focus of the Johannine text. . . . He follows the many threads of meaning, *never reaching the destination but always making progress across the difference between representation and reality*, between the sign *logos* and the One who is signified." R. R. Reno, *In the Ruins of the Church* (Grand Rapids: Brazos, 2002), 176–77. Emphasis mine.

6. Ben Bag-Bag, *Mishnah Avot* 5:22.

notion of the past. Contemporary critic George Steiner advocates approaching a text with an attitude of "radical generosity," with an expectation or trust that "there is 'something there' to be understood."[7] He is speaking about reading serious texts, good literature of any kind, and not about reading Scripture in particular. The fact that he cannot readily be charged with pietism makes his statement a useful point of departure for considering the multiple senses that may be found in the biblical text. Steiner argues further:

> We must read as if the text before us had meaning. This will not be a single meaning if the text is a serious one, if it makes us answerable to its force of life. It will not be a meaning or *figura* (structure, complex) of meanings isolated from the transformative and reinterpretative pressures of historical and cultural change. It will not be a meaning arrived at by any determinant or automatic process of cumulation and consensus. . . . Above all, the meaning striven towards will never be one which exegesis, commentary, translation, paraphrase, psychoanalytic or sociological decoding, can ever exhaust, can ever define as total. *Only weak poems can be exhaustively interpreted or understood. Only in trivial or opportunistic texts is the sum of significance that of the parts.*[8]

One implication of Steiner's argument is that no one can ever be wholly and exclusively "right" about what a text means. Even if you have managed to produce a satisfactory reading *this* time, you can never be finished with reading and interpreting even this particular passage. "Things are never used up"—thus Gerhard von Rad identifies a pattern of perpetually unfolding meaning within the structure of Old Testament narrative and prophecy, so that what seems to be the fulfillment of God's Word in one context "gives rise, all unexpected, to the promise of yet greater things. . . . Here nothing carries its ultimate meaning in itself, but is ever the earnest of yet greater wonders."[9] The insight that the literary structure of the Bible itself suggests the inexhaustibility of the words and promises of God is the warrant for the preacher's assumption that the

---

7. George Steiner, *After Babel: Aspects of Language and Translation* (Oxford: Oxford University Press, 1975), 296.

8. George Steiner, *Real Presences*, Leslie Stephen Memorial Lecture, 1 November 1985 (Cambridge: Cambridge University Press, 1986), 18. Emphasis mine.

9. Gerhard von Rad, "Typological Interpretation of the Old Testament," in *Essays on Old Testament Hermeneutics*, ed. Claus Westermann (Atlanta: John Knox, 1963), 34.

text must have something in it for us, the people of God, in whatever situation we now find ourselves.

IMAGINATIVE PRECISION

Even if we embrace the assumption that a text holds more than one meaning, it does not then follow (the most extreme forms of postmodernism notwithstanding) that we are free to ascribe meaning arbitrarily or idiosyncratically. Like all other practitioners of the applied arts, biblical interpreters and preachers must submit their work to standards of precision and functionality as well as those of imagination and beauty. As shorthand for work that meets those several standards of excellence, I shall speak of "imaginative precision."[10] Interpreters who work with imaginative precision will produce readings of the biblical text that are neither predictable nor obvious, yet ring true to those who take the time to ponder them. And—what is far more than bare truthfulness—those readings discover a truth in the text that addresses our genuine need. They show how the world of Scripture offers clarity and comfort to people who are confused by the news of the day, burdened and sometimes overwhelmed by the demands they face, the deprivations and losses they suffer.

Reading the Old Testament with imaginative precision requires a willingness to be caught off guard by a text that is sometimes amazingly blunt, that can blast through accustomed notions about God and our place in the world that God has made. Yet at the same time, they affirm that the Old Testament in all its parts speaks to us in ways that are Christianly coherent, guiding us toward an intimate yet unsentimental relationship with the God whom Christians know best as the Father of our Lord Jesus Christ. More specifically, imaginatively precise readings are likely to see correspondences between ancient social contexts and contemporary ones, to discover connections among various elements of the astonishingly intricate literary complex that is the Bible, connections that freshen and deepen the meaning of a passage, even if we have read or heard it dozens of times before.

10. Nicholas Lash, discussing the nature of imagination, makes a similar distinction: "[T]he appropriate exercise of imagination is, as every novelist knows, as strenuous, costly and ascetic an enterprise as is any other intellectually and morally responsible use of the human mind. The poet is as impatient of imprecision, as constrained by that of which he seeks to speak, as is the historian or the physicist. In every field of discourse, practical or theoretical, literary or scientific, the quest for appropriate speech is a quest for precision that is fearful of illusion. . . . Instead of contrasting 'reason' and 'imagination,' I should prefer to suggest that *imagination is the intellect in quest of appropriate precision.*" Lash, "Interpretation and Imagination," in *Incarnation and Myth: The Debate Continued,* ed. Michael Goulder (Grand Rapids: Eerdmans, 1979), 21. Italics in original.

There is, of course, no prescription for achieving imaginative precision in interpretation. However, reading the text in light of traditional modes of exegesis as well as modern methods of historical and literary analysis is a great if not indispensable help toward the goal of using the religious imagination more effectively. This is because traditional theology (the best of which is always based on careful biblical exegesis) makes fuller use of the intellect than do many forms of modern interpretation. Like other forms of traditional art, traditional biblical interpretation depends for its excellence on "an impressive amount of science":[11] careful observation about the literary structure of a biblical book, for instance, or the way a particular word is used in various places.[12] Yet it enlists the aesthetic faculty alongside the rational; it engages us in nondiscursive as well as discursive modes of thought. In the remainder of this essay, I offer examples of sermons (some of them my own) that draw on traditional modes of biblical interpretation, in each case looking for the ways in which use of the tradition may have helped the sermon achieve some degree of imaginative precision in reading and applying an Old Testament text.

It is often the case that when we encounter a work of traditional biblical interpretation, something strikes us as just right, as fitting, as beautiful—although we may not have ready words for why that is the case. And so it stays with us, as something beautiful often does, working on our imagination in mostly hidden ways until eventually it changes our own way of reading the Bible. This was my experience of the early Greek association between the *Theotokos* (Mary the God-bearer) and the burning bush. That association may originate with Gregory of Nyssa, who compares the miracle of Mary's perpetual virginity to the miracle of the bush that burns yet is not consumed.[13] But the iconographers, the monks who were both traditional artists and theologians, took it up, and thus the association of the Virgin Mary with the burning bush entered deeply into the theological imagination of the Eastern Church. Mary, pregnant or with her child, is often portrayed surrounded by the flaming bush; at times her body and clothing seem to merge with its branches.[14]

I first learned of the association between Mary and the burning bush from a student who had heard it mentioned in a lecture as an example of

11. Nasr, *Knowledge and the Sacred*, 265.
12. The sermon by John Donne in this volume offers good examples of this kind of technical expertise exercised in the reading of Scripture. See there notes 27 and 84.
13. Gregory of Nyssa, *Oratio in diem natalem Christi* (PG 46:1135–36).
14. Multiple examples of the image in several media (mosaics, icons, gold embroideries) are shown in *Sinai: Treasures of the Monastery of Saint Catherine*, ed. Konstantinos Manafis (Athens: Ekdotike Athenon, 1990), 15, 84, 172, 191, 243, 247.

"pre-critical" exegesis and wondered if it had some validity. The idea lodged in my mind, although I did not have occasion to work out its exegetical implications until some time later, when the third chapter of Exodus showed up in the lectionary on a day I was scheduled to preach.[15] The brilliance of the association lies in the fact that it brings together the seminal moments from each of the Testaments: the Sinai covenant and the incarnation. Sinai and incarnation represent God's fullest self-revelation, first to Israel alone and then to the whole world, and doubtless that is why the burning bush account is read during the Epiphany season. But drawing together those two moments in an image of pregnancy and motherhood suggests moreover that God's self-revelation is an act of the most intense intimacy—and further, a generative act, literally giving life to Israel, the church, and the world. And so it follows that Mary and Moses stand out in the Bible as the two "merely human" figures whom God seems (frankly) to love most, and in shockingly intimate ways.[16]

The fact that there is a real correspondence between Moses and Mary, between Sinai and incarnation, is borne out also by close exegesis of Exodus 3. When Moses "turns aside" to see the wondrous sight, he hears the divine voice for the first time: "I have indeed seen the affliction of my people in Egypt, and I have heard their cry. . . . Yes, I know their sufferings, and I have come down to deliver them from the power of Egypt and to bring them up to a land that is good and broad, flowing with milk and honey" (Exod. 3:7–8). I have seen, I have heard, I have come down to deliver them and bring them up to abundant life in a land of promise—is this not the gospel in a nutshell? In other words, these two self-revelations of God are really one, separated only in time. Holding them together, we see that this is how God always "comes down" into our lives, moved beyond all reason by love and by pain. Thus the image of Mary standing at the place of revelation, at Sinai, enables us to perceive the deep unity between the two Testaments. The conviction of that unity is itself a fundament of traditional exegesis.

It was the *beauty* of that association that stayed with me and eventually generated my own exegetical work. This experience affirms an understanding that is shared by all traditional interpreters of Scripture yet seems far removed from contemporary criticism: that there is an aesthetic to biblical interpretation. If we rightly perceive the truth of Scripture, then we will be moved by its beauty. Moreover, the beauty of

---

15. The resulting sermon appears in my *Getting Involved with God: Rediscovering the Old Testament* (Cambridge, Mass.: Cowley, 2001), 45–49.
16. See especially Exod. 33:17–34:8.

Scripture consists not only in its literary quality, to which many recent studies have alerted us, but also in the theological meaning it conveys. If that is right, then there is an important inference to be drawn by preachers. The beauty and therefore the power of preaching depend only in part—and not the largest part—on the rhetorical choices made for a given sermon. Rather, the aesthetic impact of the sermon depends greatly on the way we do the exegesis.

Hugh of St. Victor, in his *Didascalicon*, a highly influential treatise on the traditional arts written at the dawn of the medieval renaissance in the European church, highlights the aesthetic dimension of scriptural interpretation. Hugh compares exegesis to another traditional art, namely, stone masonry.[17] As a twelfth-century monk, Hugh understood that Scripture has multiple senses; on top of the foundation of rough stone laid in the earth, which is the literal or historical sense, the wall has several courses above ground. The upper layers are the elements of a spiritual understanding—allegorical, moral, anagogical—and these will stand only if they are firmly laid on the base of the literal sense. But a mason building a wall is working for beauty as well as strength. The upper courses of stone, unlike the subterranean base, must be polished and closely fitted if the superstructure is to be smoothly proportioned. To translate the metaphor: the several senses not only must be developed but also must cohere, one with another, if the cumulative result of interpretation ("the whole of divinity") is to clarify the church's faith. Therefore, the skilled labor of the "mason" involves finding just the right piece to juxtapose with the others, trimming and shaping each stone, each nugget of insight. The stonemason is an effective analogue to the traditional interpreter, who reckons with the roughness of Scripture, the multiple difficulties that even the most sophisticated reader must acknowledge, and yet produces a coherent reading: one that course by course, layer by layer takes account of the crucial elements of Christian faith, even if it does not explain all its mysteries.

Hugh offers the analogy of the mason as part of a larger discussion of what constitutes good judgment in allegorical interpretation.[18] Thus my

17. Hugh of St. Victor, *Didascalicon* 6.4 (*The Didascalicon of Hugh of St. Victor*, trans. Jerome Taylor [New York: Columbia University Press, 1961], 139–42). Similarly, Hugh compares exegesis to the handling of a stringed instrument (*Didascalicon* 5.2; Taylor, 120–21). The sweet sound produced by the strings (the spiritual sense) is made possible because the strings are held taut by the wood (the literal sense). The relevance of Hugh's work for biblical study was brought to my attention by Boyd Taylor Coolman, "*Pulchrum Esse:* The Exegesis of Beauty and the Art of Exegesis in Hugh of St. Victor," *Traditio* 58 (2003): 175–200.

18. "I wish you to know, good student, that this pursuit demands not slow and dull perceptions but matured mental abilities which, in the course of their searching, may so restrain their subtlety as not to lose good judgment in what they discern. Such food is solid stuff, and, unless it be well chewed, it cannot be swallowed." Hugh of St. Victor, *Didascalicon* 6.4 (Taylor, 139).

argument for Christian preaching as a traditional art touches on what may be the thorniest question of biblical hermeneutics, namely, the question of christological interpretation of the Hebrew Scriptures. Does it violate their literary, historical, and above all their theological integrity to read and preach them as pointing to and illumining the person, work, death, and resurrection of Jesus the Christ? My short answer is no. The freedom to make that move and the ability to make it with some precision are gifts that come to us out of the theological tradition, and it is essential that we continue to exercise them in preaching that takes the full measure of the gospel. But that does not mean that every sermon must or should be explicitly christological. The freedom to preach Old Testament texts christologically is, in my judgment, just that: a freedom that the Christian preacher may exercise at any time and should exercise sometimes, not a requirement for preaching any particular text responsibly. Yet even if we are free to interpret thus, our interpretations are nonetheless subject to critique. The criterion of imaginative precision involves close attention to what happens to a part of Israel's Scripture when we listen to it specifically in the context of Jesus' story. If an allegorical approach is warranted in a given instance, then I think we should be able to identify, in the text and also in the situation of preaching, what it is that invites such an approach. In the several examples that follow, the warrant is somewhat different in each case.

READING "AROUND CHRIST"

The first example is from the seventeenth-century Anglican Puritan bishop Joseph Hall, from his *Contemplations on the Historical Passages of the Old and New Testament*, the remarkable series of short exegetical essays that Hall described as "the ore mined from my sermons."[19] His text is the story of Absalom's rebellion and death, when David utters his famous lament: "My son Absalom, my son, my son Absalom! If only I had died in your stead, Absalom, my son, my son" (2 Sam. 19:1 [18:33 Eng.]). We are so accustomed to being moved by David's abject grief that we forget also to be puzzled by it—after all, David went to war against his son, and it was to be presumed that one of them would die. In more than one place, the biblical narrator shows us the logical inconsistency of David's fighting an enemy for whom his strongest feeling is tender love.

---

19. See the essay on Hall and several of the Contemplations in Ellen F. Davis, *Imagination Shaped: Old Testament Preaching in the Anglican Tradition* (Valley Forge, Pa.: Trinity Press International, 1995), 114–57.

With his extreme sensitivity to the dynamics of biblical narrative, Bishop Hall sees in that inconsistency a clue to the deeper logic at work in the text. This is his comment when David musters his troops and, "encourag[ing] them by his eye, and restrain[ing] them with his tongue," gives one final battle instruction: "Deal gently with the young man Absalom for my sake" (2 Sam. 18:5):

> How unreasonably favourable are the wars of a father! O holy David, what means this ill-placed love, this unjust mercy? Deal gently with a traitor! but of all traitors with a son! of all sons with an Absalom, the graceless darling of so good a father; and all this "for my sake," whose crown, whose blood he hunts after! For whose sake should Absalom be pursued, if he must be forborne for thine?[20]

Hall at first seems to lean toward a plain-sense reading, that David's instruction bespeaks merely the same fatherly indulgence that produced such a rotten child: "Even in the holiest parents nature may be guilty of an injurious tenderness, of a bloody indulgence."[21] But then, and without ever abandoning that good literal interpretation, he argues for a reading that makes sense at another level:

> Or, whether shall we not rather think this was done in type of that unmeasurable mercy of the true king, and redeemer of Israel, who prayed for his persecutors, for his murderers; and, even while they were at once scorning and killing him, could say, "Father, forgive them, for they know not what they do." If we be sons, we are ungracious, we are rebellious, yet still is our heavenly father thus compassionately regardful of us. . . . As for us, we are never but under mercy; our God needs no advantages to sweep us from the earth any moment, yet he continues that life, and those powers to us, whereby we provoke him, and bids his angels deal kindly with us, and bear us in their arms, while we lift up our hands, and bend our tongues against heaven. O mercy past the comprehension of all finite spirits, and only to be conceived by him whose it is: never more resembled by any earthly affection, than by this of his deputy and type, "Deal gently with the young man Absalom for my sake."[22]

20. Joseph Hall, *Contemplations* 16.3 (*Contemplations on the Historical Passages of the Old and New Testament* [1833; repr., Morgan, Pa.: Soli Deo Gloria, 1995], 2:65).
21. Ibid.
22. Ibid., 2:65–66.

To appreciate this reading of David as a type of Christ, it is important to understand that Hall was not, like the medieval preachers who preceded him by a few generations, a habitual allegorist. Reared in a Puritan home in the last quarter of the sixteenth century, he fully shared the Reformers' commitment to literal reading. (Doubtless Hall would agree with Hugh of St. Victor that no true student of Scripture resorts to allegory just to get around something he does not understand.)[23] What causes him to make that move here is the kind of observation that only someone keenly attentive to the dynamics of biblical narrative could make. He discovers in the narrative logic what George Steiner would call an "ontological difficulty."[24] An ontological difficulty resides in the essential meaning of a poem or story; it is not going to be resolved when a reader has secured more information or figured out some confusion in the plot. Therefore, an ontological difficulty, as Andrew Louth comments, "demand[s] of the reader a radical reorientation as to what meaning is at all. It is not trying to say anything we might anticipate: rather it is trying to call into question our very anticipations. . . . [O]ntological difficulty is something very like the mysterious—there is no answer, only engagement."[25] Thus when the biblical narrator places so much stress on David's passionate concern for his rebellious son— understandable in a father, yet illogical under the conditions of this war—Hall perceives that we are being drawn to another level of logic. Better, perhaps: we are being drawn into a mystery. Finally, we must see this logic as divine rather than human and this emotion as an indication of God's unimaginable compassion for us—a compassion expressed most fully, as the Christian imagination reads the Bible, in the cross.[26]

It is instructive to compare Hall's work with a volume of essays edited by Claus Westermann about forty years ago, in which a group of German biblical scholars (including Gerhard von Rad, Martin Noth, and Hans Walter Wolff) argued for a renewed appreciation of typology as an

---

23. Hugh of St. Victor, *Didascalicon* 6.10 (Taylor, 148).

24. See George Steiner, *On Difficulty; and Other Essays* (Oxford: Oxford University Press, 1978), 18–47.

25. Andrew Louth, *Discerning the Mystery: An Essay on the Nature of Theology* (Oxford: Clarendon, 1983), 111. Using terms posed by George Steiner, Louth goes on to observe that allegory as a response to the "difficulty" of the Scriptures "is not a way of obfuscation, as it would be if allegory were a device for solving 'contingent' difficulties: rather allegory is a way of holding us before the mystery which is the ultimate 'difficulty' of the Scriptures—a difficulty, a mystery, which challenges us to revise our understanding of what might be meant by meaning; a difficulty, a mystery, which calls on us for a response of *metanoia*, change of mental perspective, repentance. . . . It is important to realize this: that the traditional doctrine of the multiple sense of Scripture, with its use of allegory, is essentially an attempt to respond to the *mira profunditas* of Scripture, seen as the indispensable witness to the mystery of Christ" (111–12).

26. As Peter Hawkins points out (personal communication), a nonchristological—yet still figural, or allegorical—reading of this text might see it as pointing to God's compassion for "Israel, my son" (cf. Exod. 4:22–23; Hos. 11:1).

approach to Old Testament hermeneutics.[27] In general, the essayists want to distinguish typology from allegory and discredit the latter, in accordance with the general tendency of scholarship in the latter half of the twentieth century, under the influence of Jean Daniélou.[28] However, in these essays the positive alternative never emerges clearly, as the several authors do not agree on the basis for typological representation. For example, Noth maintains that "a legitimate 're-presentation' cannot use the individual human figures of biblical history as its subjects," nor "specific historical situations which emerge in the Old Testament"; rather, "the subject of a legitimate 're-presentation' can only be the saving acts of God himself."[29] On the other hand, Wolff asserts: "The great majority of Old Testament texts offer not typical model cases of God's people, but a colorful variety of ways, deeds, decisions, and sufferings of God's people, *nothing but individual situations of Israel and of men.*" Therefore, and apparently in direct disagreement with Noth, Wolff argues that typology "is most vitally interested in *just these concrete historical facts.*"[30]

The collection of essays fails not only to set forth clear criteria for what constitutes good typological exegesis but also to point to any concrete examples, either classical or contemporary. The scholar or preacher who would like to try typological interpretation of an actual text is left guessing. By contrast, Joseph Hall, active as both liturgical preacher and scholar for the first half of the seventeenth century, consistently demonstrates an imaginatively precise treatment of large segments of biblical narrative. Hall's *Contemplations*, still in print after four hundred years, bear comparison with the expository works of Luther and Calvin. Although the commentaries of the Reformers are based on their sermons, the leisurely discursive style generally seems (at least to moderns) far removed from the pulpit—unlike the prose of the *Contemplations*, which has the concision and crispness of poetry. These are arguably, then, the most useful model extant of a Christian preacher's efforts to

27. Claus Westermann, ed., *Essays on Old Testament Hermeneutics* (Atlanta: John Knox, 1963). Von Rad's essay is cited above (note 9).

28. In a lucid essay, Frances Young offers a critical evaluation of "the Daniélou definition of typology," which, she maintains, has seriously distorted "what the ancients were doing in their exegesis." Daniélou contrasted typology, which shows that "the same divine characteristics are revealed in successive strata of history," with allegory, seen as "a recrudescence of nature-symbolism, from which the element of historicity is absent." Young asserts that this "critical orthodoxy" cannot be maintained, partly because the Fathers did not in fact have a term corresponding to "typology," and further because, with respect to the distinction Daniélou makes, "in most texts the one shades into the other almost indistinguishably." Young, "Typology," in *Crossing the Boundaries*, ed. Stanley Porter, Paul Joyce, and David Orton (Leiden: Brill, 1994), 34, 31, 33.

29. Martin Noth, "The 'Re-presentation' of the Old Testament in Proclamation," in Westermann, *Essays on Old Testament Hermeneutics*, 86–87.

30. Hans Walter Wolff, "The Hermeneutics of the Old Testament," in Westermann, *Essays on Old Testament Hermeneutics*, 196–97. Emphasis mine.

uphold both the literal sense and the unity of the two Testaments within a literarily and theologically sophisticated reading of large portions of the Bible.

The example from Hall illustrates how an allegorical reading—or, to use the term currently more popular, a figural[31] reading—may be motivated by a problem in understanding the logic of the text. My next example, from one of my own sermons,[32] reflects a move to allegory in order to achieve a different kind of precision, namely, to make an accurate connection between the text and the audience, who on this occasion were my students and faculty colleagues at the Virginia Theological Seminary. The liturgical setting was a Eucharist and healing service during the fourth week of Lent, and I chose for my text Psalm 39, one of only two lament psalms that end in complete desolation (cf. Ps. 88), with no turning toward or anticipation of praise. In the *Book of Common Prayer* translation we used for that service, the final lines are these:

> Turn your gaze from me, that I may be glad again,
>   before I go my way and am no more.

My original intention had been straightforward. The psalmist is obviously depressed, and so I tried (for some days) to write a sermon about depression as it is experienced by people of faith, reminding the congregation that some among us would still be cast down several weeks hence, even while the church as a whole would be entering the Easter season. My exegesis seemed all right, but the tone was completely wrong. The first draft of that sermon was "preachy" in the worst sense: overly anecdotal and therefore intrusive, theologically superficial and therefore moralistic. Stalled at this dead end, I happened to read Andrew Louth's discussion of the multiple senses of Scripture, as traditional interpreters beginning with Origen reckoned them. His major point is that the *order* of the senses is intentional and theologically significant. For Augustine, Gregory the Great, and most of the Later Fathers, it is crucial that the allegorical sense precede the so-called moral sense. That is, we must read the Old Testament text in relation to the story of Jesus *before* we can discover its meaning for the Christian life. Louth argues that if we first read the text allegorically, then the moral reading that follows denotes a

---

31. See, for instance, Christopher Seitz, *Figured Out: Typology and Providence in Christian Scripture* (Louisville, Ky.: Westminster John Knox, 2001); and John David Dawson, *Christian Figural Reading and the Fashioning of Identity* (Berkeley: University of California Press, 2002).

32. The sermon discussed here appears in Ellen F. Davis and Richard B. Hays, eds., *The Art of Reading Scripture* (Grand Rapids: Eerdmans, 2003), 300–305.

movement of response and fulfillment. As the church, we are called to recognize and live in response to the God who meets us in history, who has already met us through covenant and incarnation.[33]

That insight from Louth enabled me to identify my problem: I was trying to embed the psalm directly in the narratives of my listeners' lives (as least as I imagined their lives), and it was resisting. But the liturgical calendar—an indispensable aid to traditional interpretation—was offering me another narrative context that I was ignoring. The Gospel passage appointed was from the fourteenth chapter of Mark, Jesus' prayer and arrest at Gethsemane. In that context, the psalm, with its anguished lament over the brevity and (perhaps) the futility of human life, read like a script for Jesus' "agitated" (Mark 14:33 NRSV) prayer. As the psalm expresses no assurance that God has heard or will ever hear, so the Gethsemane scene ends with Jesus' arrest, his prayer for deliverance apparently unheeded. Moreover, following the Fathers in giving priority to the allegorical meaning, I saw new depth in what may be the most striking line in the prayer: כִּי גֵר אָנֹכִי עִמָּךְ (kî ger ʾanokhî ʿimmakh), "For I am a resident alien with you [God], like all my ancestors" (Ps. 39:13 [12 Eng.]). Thus the psalmist establishes her pedigree; she takes her place in a long line of resident aliens in the household of God. Reading that line in light of the Gospel puts a new perspective on the suffering psalmist's claim to be a resident alien with God. In the person of Jesus Christ, God became a resident alien: alien to humanity, rejected by us—and for a time, on the cross, Jesus is alien even to God.

Further, reading the psalm "around Christ"[34] proved to be the key to the moral sense of the text—that is, it enabled me to make the connection between the text and the experience of the listeners. By keeping the focus on Christ, I was able to move beyond speaking "sympathetically" about the depression experienced by Christians. I could see it for what it really is, understood theologically: participation in the real, historical suffering of Christ (Phil. 3:10; 1 Pet. 4:13; cf. 2 Cor. 1:5–7). Afterward, one of my students, who had long suffered from chronic depression, commented, "For the first time I can begin to make sense of the whole of my life in light of my faith." *Allegoriâ crescimus*, "By means of allegory, we grow."[35]

---

33. Louth, *Discerning the Mystery*, 115–17.

34. Rowan Williams observes, "We need to read the Bible around Christ, and read it, therefore, in the confidence that our own mishearing and misapprehending, our own confusions and uncertainties about the text and about the matter with which it deals, will be part of God's triumphant work in us." Williams, "Reading the Bible," in *A Ray of Darkness* (Cambridge, Mass.: Cowley, 1995), 136.

35. Hugh of Rouen, quoted in Louth, *Discerning the Mystery*, 120.

TRADITION AND INNOVATION

My final example addresses the question that any appeal to traditional interpretation must meet, namely, how does something genuinely new enter the theological tradition? Can a traditional approach encourage new thought, or is it simply a cover-up for a desire to maintain the *status quo,* or perhaps to recover the *status quo ante*? The key to answering that challenge is the function of the imagination. For traditional interpretation makes fuller use of the imagination than do most forms of modern criticism—an important fact, if indeed the hallmark of good exegesis is "imaginative precision." Moreover, it makes more theologically disciplined use of the imagination than do some forms of postmodernism, as well as many contemporary sermons. I want to suggest that a robust imagination, schooled in the ways of Christian theology, is indispensable for the emergence of fruitful innovation in the church's thought.

In an important recent study, *Tradition and Imagination,* David Brown takes issue with the view, common to Enlightenment writers and their heirs, that tradition is essentially bondage to and infatuation with the past.[36] On the contrary, Brown maintains that a healthy tradition (in his term, an "open" tradition) actively conduces to innovation. This is true, first, because "the imagination works by building upon tradition."[37] Especially a religious tradition, with its multiple forms of artistic expression, provides food for the imagination that is rich but not raw. Second, it is the very function of the imagination "to challenge, not to reinforce conformity" and established assumptions. A multifaceted tradition serves to free the imagination from the inevitable narrowness of our current mindset: "As we look back over the centuries, . . . the effective artist then becomes one who enables us to comprehend very different assumptions and values from our own."[38] Therefore, interpretation practiced as a traditional art pursues a middle course between modernism and postmodernism. Over against modernism, it maintains that we can interpret a text only as we

---

36. Brown cites the first line of Kant's 1784 essay *Was ist Aufklärung?* in which he "defines enlightenment as freedom from any form of intellectual dependence on another: *der Ausgang des Menschen aus seiner selbstverschuldeten Unmündigkeit* [the emancipation of humanity from its self-incurred immaturity]." David Brown, *Tradition and Imagination: Revelation and Change* (Oxford: Oxford University Press, 1999), 25 n. 52. Among contemporary biblical scholars, André LaCocque offers a sustained critique of tradition as idealization of the past designed to maintain domination in the present. He reads the Song of Songs as being itself a subversion of tradition; it is "a defiant, irreverent, subversive discourse" that makes ironic use of the language of earlier biblical writers, and especially the prophets, in order to issue a protest against a patriarchal worldview and "the prevailing mentalities of the late second temple period." He argues further that the traditional allegorical interpretation of the church has served through millennia to disguise the subversive character of the text and reinforce the values it seeks to undermine. LaCocque, *Romance, She Wrote: A Hermeneutical Essay on Song of Songs* (Harrisburg, Pa.: Trinity Press International, 1998), 12, 17.
37. Brown, *Tradition and Imagination,* 40.
38. Ibid., 28.

are aware of how our own situation and the deeply rooted perspectives that belong to it may shape our reading. Over against postmodernism, it contends that our present outlook, isolated from earlier perspectives, is an inadequate basis for theological understanding.[39] In contrast to both of these, active involvement in a viable religious tradition contributes to the development of the profound and far-reaching historical consciousness that is indispensable for understanding the account of intermingled divine and human life that is the biblical story.

Hans-Georg Gadamer's comment on valuing the element of tradition in a hermeneutic of the human sciences is apt:

> At the beginning of all historical hermeneutics, then, the abstract antithesis between tradition and historical research, between history and knowledge, must be discarded. The effect of a living tradition and the effect of historical study must constitute a unity, the analysis of which would reveal only a texture of reciprocal relationships. Hence we would do well not to regard historical consciousness as something radically new—as it seems at first—but as a new element within that which has always made up the human relation to the past. In other words, we have to recognise the element of tradition in the historical relation and enquire into its hermeneutical productivity.[40]

About a dozen years ago, I received a preaching assignment that required me to take an explicitly traditional approach to an Old Testament text. During the season of Lent, the chapel staff of Yale Divinity School commissioned a series of sermons on images of Christ in the Old Testament. The sermon I contributed, the first self-consciously "allegorical" sermon I had ever preached, is relevant to the question of tradition and innovation because it proved to be a turning point in my theological thinking. In it I began to articulate what has since become an important dimension of my biblical and theological work: interpreting Scripture, and especially the Old Testament, in light of the current ecological crisis. If David Brown is right, that tradition conduces to innovation, then it may be more than coincidence that this particular assignment led me to exercise my exegetical and theological imagination in a new way—that is, in a way that is distinctly innovative from the perspective of my professional training as a biblical scholar.

39. Ibid., 6.
40. Hans-Georg Gadamer, *Truth and Method* (New York: Seabury, 1975), 251.

For my text I chose a passage from Isaiah 63, one that has a venerable history of christological reading during Lent:

> Who is this coming from Edom,
> in crimson-stained garments from Bozrah . . . ?
> "It is I, speaking in righteousness,
> powerful to save."
> Why is your clothing now red,
> your garments like one who treads in the winepress?
> "I trod a vintage alone,
> and from the nations, no one was with me.
> And I trod them in my anger,
> and trampled them in my wrath,
> and their life-blood spattered on my garments,
> and all my clothing was stained.
> For a day of vengeance was in my heart. . . .
> My own arm worked victory for me,
> and my wrath sustained me."
>
> *(Isa. 63:1–5)*[41]

I chose the "grapes of wrath" passage because for centuries the Book of Common Prayer appointed it to be read on the Monday of Holy Week[42]—until good taste, or squeamishness, prevailed. Now God-in-Christ no longer appears as a blood-spattered warrior during the most important week of the Christian year. I chose the passage also because I suspected that the language of divine rage could instruct us in that season of the year in a way that softer words could not. The whole book of Isaiah, including this final postexilic portion, shows us a picture of God burning with an anger stoked hot by love. That image accords with the gospel (e.g., Matt. 25:24–30, 41–46; John 2:14–17; Rev. 2:4–5, 19–23), and therefore such an image surely has a place in our religious imaginations, especially in the season of penitence. As I dwelt on the peculiar intensity of Isaiah's representation of the Divine Warrior, it occurred to me that the best contemporary application of it might be not to our

---

41. The parallel passage in Isa. 59:15–17 reinforces the interpretation of the prophetic image as evoking Christ's triumph over sin and death:

And [YHWH] saw that there was no man,
and he was aghast that no one intervened.
But his own arm worked deliverance for him. (v. 16)

42. The practice of reading the passage during Holy Week was taken from the Roman Catholic Church. In the Roman and Sarum missals, Isa. 62:11–63:7 was appointed for Wednesday of Holy Week. Beginning in 1549, the passage was appointed for Monday of Holy Week in both the English and American versions of the Book of Common Prayer. It is omitted in the 1979 *Book of Common Prayer* (American).

individual sins but rather to the sin of ecological devastation, currently perpetrated, with still-accelerating force, by our society as a whole. Isaiah is not, after all, focusing primarily on the sins of individuals but the sins of whole nations—at different times, the foreign nations and Israel itself—who have exalted themselves at the expense of God's glory, and also at the expense of the weak (e.g., Isa. 63:6).

Another seventeenth-century preacher, George Herbert (whose sermons, sadly, were not preserved),[43] helped me draw the connection more carefully between Isaiah's Divine Warrior and Christ's passion, in which divine rage at sin and hot-burning love are likewise inseparably intermingled. In his poem "The Agony," Herbert offers a reading of Christ's bloody sweat in Gethsemane (Luke 22:44) that evokes also Isaiah's image of treading out the bloody vintage—although for Herbert, it is God-in-Christ who is caught in the press:

> Who would know Sin, let him repair
> Unto Mount Olivet; there shall he see
> A man so wrung with pains, that all his hair,
>   His skin, his garments bloody be.
> Sin is that press and vice, which forceth pain
> To hunt his cruel food through ev'ry vein.
>
> . . . .
>
> Love is that liquor sweet and most divine,
> Which my God feels as blood; but I, as wine.[44]

The central point of "application" for my sermon was that meditating on the scriptural images of an angry, loving, and blood-stained God should awaken us to share the divine rage—and agony—at our collective sin of despising God's creation. In other words, the sermon was a call to repentance, which I characterized as a "headlong run into God's anger" with the intention of being "changed at any cost." We must offer ourselves

> for the change that will enable future generations also to know
> the world as a lovely and livable place. We are called to follow
> Christ in meeting force with force, the force of greedy destruc-
> tion with the force of our own willing sacrifice. For Christ's sac-
> rifice does not take the place of our own—and that is the single

43. Although Herbert's sermons (from his few years as rector of two rural parishes) were not preserved, his view of the preacher's role—and to some extent of "his" method—are memorably presented in *A Priest to the Temple; or The Country Parson*, Herbert's classic portrayal of the faithful pastor's life and practice.

44. George Herbert, "The Agonie," in *The Temple* (published posthumously in 1633), repr., "The Agony," in *The Country Parson, The Temple*, by George Herbert, ed. John N. Wall Jr. (New York: Paulist Press, 1981), 151.

most crucial point for discipleship. Christ's sacrifice does not make our sacrifice unnecessary but rather makes it possible. Jesus' sacrifice on the cross teaches us how to live in this world according to the strange inverse economics of the kingdom of heaven, where wealth is measured by how much you can afford to let go, comfort level by your ease in giving up. Far from taking us off the hook, Jesus Christ challenges us to get used to the steady pain of repentance and sacrifice, to explore that difficult terrain that Christians have traditionally called "the way of the cross" and discover it to be "the way of life and peace."[45]

I would now criticize what I did ten years ago as not demonstrating enough exegetical precision. Having in the interim thought much more about the theology of Isaiah, I see that there is a stronger case to be made for preaching this prophetic book in particular as a call to ecological repentance, since according to "the vision of Isaiah" (Isa. 1:1),[46] the root sin of every nation is failure to acknowledge God's sovereignty over all kingdoms *and all creation* (e.g., Isa. 40:21–28; 42:5–17; 45:1–7). Since both those aspects of divine sovereignty are affirmed by the gospel, I should have drawn a tighter connection than I did between ecology and Christology. But despite the shortcomings of my execution, I believe that the traditional cast of the preaching assignment—to render an image of Christ from the Old Testament—prompted me to begin moving into an area of thought that the church is only newly recognizing as exegetically plausible and genuinely theological.

I conclude by raising two questions that follow from this last example of Christ-centered preaching of an Old Testament text. They are questions with which any Christian preacher must, in my judgment, wrestle repeatedly, although I offer here some considerations that bear closely on my own thinking about how something timely, valuable, and perhaps new may enter Christian tradition through preaching that is imaginatively and exegetically precise. The first question returns us to where we began this study: Is it really necessary to preach from the Old Testament at all, especially if Christians may read the Old Testament explicitly as well as implicitly in light of the gospel? Perhaps the single best argument for the necessity of the Old Testament is that without it, we could not

45. The phrases come from the Collect for Monday in Holy Week: "Mercifully grant that we, walking in the way of the cross, may find it none other than the way of life and peace" (BCP, 220).
46. I consider that this phrase applies to the book as a whole, and my comments here apply to a treatment of both the eighth-century and the exilic portions of Isaiah.

understand the depth of God's involvement in our material and political existence. Through a complex history of covenant and election, Israel's Scriptures give us a long-range view of our relationship with God. They show how that relationship is ineluctably both embedded in and expressed through social practices and political institutions. Further, they give convicting demonstrations of how Israel's relationship with God, and ours, may be compromised by those practices and institutions. The Old Testament in its "worldliness" is indispensable if we are to make fresh and compelling connections between the gospel and the concrete social, political, and economic circumstances in which we live out our faith. I think it is something like this that Dietrich Bonhoeffer had in mind when he wrote, in Advent 1943: "I don't think it is Christian to want to get to the New Testament too soon and too directly. . . . You cannot and must not speak the last word before you have spoken the next to last. We live on the next to last word, and believe on the last, don't we?"[47]

The second question concerns the criteria by which our own acts of theological imagination, our current and sometimes innovative interpretations, are to be judged. From a traditional perspective, the most important function of the imagination is to discern the prompting and teaching of the Holy Spirit. One contemporary monastic theologian, Jean Leclercq, identifies the Christian tradition itself as the manifestation of the Holy Spirit; it is "the stream of life . . . coming to us through the Church from the Crucified and Glorified Christ."[48] Tradition in that sense can exist only in the stable yet dynamic environment established by active ministry and mission, worship, study, and interactive conversation about the things of God—all that ongoing from generation to generation. In such an environment, we may trust that the work of the Holy Spirit will indeed manifest itself in the periodic emergence of the radically new, which can be accepted and valued because it stands in discernible continuity with what the church has already recognized as God's work.

And what of the new interpretations that emerge in our own preaching? Probably we cannot accurately discern which of them may be judged to bespeak, however feebly, the work of the Holy Spirit in our time and place—and thus be found worthy of a permanent hearing in the tradition in which we work. But to the extent they may be so judged,

---

47. Dietrich Bonhoeffer, *Letters and Papers from Prison* (London: SCM Press, 1953), 50.
48. Jean Leclercq, "Contemporary Monasticism," *Fairacres Chronicle* 12, no. 3 (1979): 7.

it will be because they succeed to some degree in holding us still before the *mira profunditas* of Scripture, that "wondrous depth" that questions us and yet continues to reveal itself to our faithful questioning, so that we may read as those who, having once "submitted to God's surprising work in Christ, expect to be surprised again and again"[49] by these astonishing Scriptures.

---

49. From an unpublished essay by Jason Byassee, June 2002.

CHAPTER 4

Giving Sight: The Christian Artistry
of Lancelot Andrewes

Instinctively, everyone knows the difference between a "preachy" sermon and one that "preaches." At least, everyone on the listening side of the pulpit knows the difference. A preachy sermon has the same effect as any good(?) talking-to: the listeners feel judged, though perhaps not personally convicted; they have been lectured at, though not necessarily instructed. As for a sermon that *preaches*, the verb form itself is telling. The sermon—or better, the biblical text—seems to be preaching itself. The person and words of the preacher are at its disposal. They are transparent and, in a certain sense, forgettable, but through them the gospel message becomes imprinted on the minds of the listeners. When the text uses the preacher in order to be heard and believed, the words of the prophet are fulfilled: "All flesh is grass. . . . Grass withers, the flower fades, but the word of our God stands forever" (Isa. 40:6–8).

There are moments in the classroom when that kind of sermon can be sensed in the making. We are working on a biblical text, and someone says something—most often a brief observation, a sentence or two—that brings us all to attention. In a flash of illumination we know that through Scripture, God has spoken to us exactly the words we need to hear. Grateful and astonished, someone may murmur, "That'll preach." In that moment of unmistakable recognition, we have, all of us, caught a glimpse of something. You might call it a moral vision, and that is something different from a moral lesson—what one might get from being preached at. Rather, the world has suddenly opened up in a way that invites us to enter into possibilities for our existence that were not evident before. It is the difference between being beckoned forward and being pushed from behind—maybe even hammered over the head. Both might be described as forms of "guidance," but even if the latter has some beneficial effect, one is unlikely to seek it out a second time. Coercion may in some instances prove irresistible, but it is never attractive.

Krister Stendahl once memorably described the preacher's function as "giving the text a little more room to shine."[1] It sounds modest enough, yet in fact it is a more exacting moral and rhetorical task than what people generally have in mind when they use the common but vague language of "speaking with biblical authority." For the Bible is, as I have suggested, an immediate and insistent presence thrust into the center of the church's life. Anyone who reads it with alertness and honesty must recognize that it calls on each of us to submit to a process of change that is never-ending, and regularly painful. A direct demand for submission—stating the divine precept or judgment in a magisterial tone and expecting acquiescence—is unlikely to work with most congregations, at least in North America and Western Europe. Maybe it never worked well. Walter Brueggemann observes, "We now know . . . that human transformation (the way people change) does not happen through didacticism or through excessive certitude, but through the playful entertainment of another scripting of reality."[2] And in a post-Christian (or postreligious) culture, moral coercion is not just ineffective; it is hard to apply in the first place. No one is compelled by law or social necessity to go to church and listen to sermons, and increasingly few are so compelled by familial expectations. Moreover, there is no internal impetus to listen to the biblical mandate for change, since the Bible has no privileged status in a postmodern context. So preachers do not have any form of coercion on their side. In this situation, perhaps the only way to preach the biblical message faithfully is by making a compelling appeal to human freedom.

In an essay on the significance of accurate vision for the moral life, Stanley Hauerwas counters the view of freedom prevalent in Christian ethics as well as in general culture, namely, that it consists in the exercise of the will in matters of moral choice. Drawing on the work of Iris Murdoch, he argues that the moral life has more to do with *seeing accurately* than it does with making explicit moral choices—although the ability to know and do what is right is an important consequence of "the progres-

---

1. The remark was made in the course of an informal "Conversation with the Beecher Lecturer," Yale Divinity School, October 1983.
2. Walter Brueggemann, *Cadences of Home: Preaching among Exiles* (Louisville, Ky.: Westminster John Knox, 1997), 29.

sive attempt to widen and clarify our vision of reality."[3] Accordingly, freedom consists in "the disciplined overcoming of the self that allows for the clarification of our vision."[4] And further (quoting Murdoch): "Freedom is knowing and understanding and respecting things quite other than ourselves."[5]

Based on that understanding of the moral life and of human freedom, Hauerwas makes two observations that are important for my own treatment of a style of preaching that enables Christians to see more accurately. First, good and great art serves an important moral function; it "reveals to us aspects of our world that we are usually too dependent on conventionality and fantasy to be able to see."[6] Indeed, the artist at work may be seen as "the paradigm of the moral [person],"[7] for (again, quoting Murdoch) "in the creation of a work of art the artist is going through the exercise of attending to something quite particular other than himself."[8] A second observation derives from the view that freedom is the overcoming of self: "The virtue most necessary for freedom is humility," which "is not a phony attempt at constant self-effacement, but *the selfless respect for reality*."[9] In this essay I offer a portrait of the preacher as an artist who, through humble practice of the art to which she is called, clarifies the moral vision of her hearers, enabling them first to see the truth of the gospel and then to desire to meet its challenge.

PREACHING HUMILITY

As my model for that portrait I take one particular preacher: Bishop Lancelot Andrewes (1555–1626), a foundational theologian of the newly reformed Church of England, best known as a favorite preacher in the courts of Elizabeth I and James I. Andrewes was one of the most broadly learned churchmen in Europe, exceptional even in a time when scholars did not confine themselves to a single "discipline." As a student and young scholar, he mastered twenty or more ancient and modern languages. He frequently lectured on books of the Old Testament and was one of the primary translators of the Hebrew Scriptures for the Authorized (King

---

3. Stanley Hauerwas, "The Significance of Vision: Toward an Aesthetic Ethic," in *Vision and Virtue: Essays in Christian Ethical Reflection* (Notre Dame, Ind.: University of Notre Dame Press, 1981), 44.

4. Ibid., 40.

5. Ibid., 41, quoting Iris Murdoch, "The Sublime and the Beautiful Revisited," *Yale Review* 49 (1959): 269–70.

6. Hauerwas, "Significance of Vision," 39.

7. Ibid., 40.

8. Ibid., quoting Iris Murdoch, "The Sublime and the Good," *Chicago Review* 13 (1959): 54–55.

9. Hauerwas, "Significance of Vision," 40–41. Emphasis mine.

James) Version. Yet it would be a mistake to call him merely(!) a biblical scholar. His first appointment at Cambridge following ordination to the priesthood was as catechist at Pembroke Hall, where his teaching topics ranged from biblical theology to dogmatics to sacramental theology to Christian education. Many considered him the most knowledgeable liturgical scholar of the day.

In turning to Lancelot Andrewes, I am following the lead of my students. Through the years, I have recurrently assigned Andrewes' sermons in seminars that focus on exegesis for preaching. I do so because I know no other preacher so adept at teaching Christians how to read and find meaning in Scripture. In his ability as a Hebraist, his careful application of hermeneutical principles, and his fine sense of pastoral exegesis, Andrewes might be compared to Calvin, to whom he may owe some intellectual debt.[10] The precise features of his preaching text—its words, its tone, its literary setting—constitute the starting point for every thought. Andrewes takes hold of a word of Scripture and "follow[s] it hard," to use his phrase.[11] Then, choosing his own words with care, he works to bring the language and the logic of the text into direct contact with the heart and situation of the listener.

Andrewes is distinguished as a preacher not only (and perhaps not primarily) by his vast and exquisite learning but also by his artfulness. He is one of the greatest English prose stylists of any age,[12] something of which James was doubtless mindful when he gave him oversight of the translation committee responsible for Genesis through Kings—that is, virtually all the prose in the Old Testament. Andrewes' command of words and his imagination are comparable to those of his younger contemporary, John Donne. Donne's capacity to dazzle may be unmatchable, but he requires patience from his readers, frequently departing from his main point in order to pursue another idea that catches his interest. With Andrewes, "the steady march of logic and passion"[13] rarely falters from start to finish of an hour-long sermon. Indeed, it is precisely the tightness of logic and rhetoric that makes him compelling to read

10. Although Andrewes is often characterized as virulently anti-Calvinist, the points on which he seems to resemble Calvin may reflect some genuine, if indirect, influence. During Andrewes' boyhood, Calvin's authority—personal, intellectual, and ecclesial—was at its height among English clergy. Andrewes was educated by a "warm Protestant," Richard Mulcaster, headmaster at Merchant Taylors' School in London, and "at Cambridge he was attracted to the devotional side of Calvinism." Douglas Macleane, *Lancelot Andrewes and the Reaction* (London: George Allen & Sons, 1910), 44, 52.

11. Thus Andrewes describes the literary style of the Apostle Paul in 1 Cor. 15:20–58. Lancelot Andrewes, Easter 1607, in *Ninety-Six Sermons*, ed. J. P. Wilson (Oxford: J. H. Parker, 1841–1843; reprinted from the second edition, 1631), 2:213. All subsequent references to Andrewes' sermons are to this edition.

12. See T. S. Eliot's classic essay "Lancelot Andrewes" (1926), reprinted in *Selected Essays, 1917–1932* (London: Faber & Faber, 1932), 317–29.

13. F. P. Wilson, *Seventeenth Century Prose* (Cambridge: Cambridge University Press, 1960), 99.

and hard to quote. But what marks Andrewes' art as unique is the fact that the images that fill his mind derive directly and exclusively from the words of Scripture. Each word can be treated as a deliberate and significant choice of the Holy Ghost. A word from God is a spiritual reality, an irreducible communicator of some specific aspect of the Divine Mystery. The words may be translated (although Andrewes never lets us forget that the English is but a translation); however, they can no more be replaced by substitutes or abstractions than can the elements of bread and wine to which Andrewes regularly alludes. "His nominals be reals," he observes in the well-known Nativity sermon of 1614.[14]

In this case, it is the Hebrew "nominal" *Immanuel* ("with us is God") that leads more deeply into the reality of God. Working with Hebrew and Latin interchangeably, Andrewes dissects the compound word and thus unfolds its significance for his multilingual auditors:

> Though *El* ["God"] be the more principal, yet I cannot tell whether it or *Immanu* ["with us"] do more concern us. For as in *El* is might, so in *Immanu* is our right to his might, and to all he hath or is worth. By that word we hold, therefore we to lay hold of it. The very standing of it thus before, thus in the first place, toucheth us somewhat. . . .
>
> Good manners would in a name compound of him and us, that he should have stood before us, and it have been *Elimmanu* at least—*Deus nobiscum*, and *Deus* before *nobiscum*; not Immanuel, *nobiscum* before *Deus*. . . . But he giving it himself would have it stand thus; us set before him. There is a meaning in it. And what can it be but this? That in the very name we might read that we are dearer to him than himself; that he so preferred us, and that his own name doth *prae se ferre* ["manifest itself"] no less, but give out to all the world the *ecce* of St. John's Gospel, *Ecce quomodo dilexit!* . . . "See how he loved them!" (John 11:36). . . . See it in his very name. We are a part of it; we are the forepart of it, and he the latter. He behind, and we before—before himself, and that by order from himself; he would have it Immanuel. O, whether was greater, humility or charity in him! Hard to say whether, but both unspeakable.[15]

14. Andrewes, Christmas 1614, 1:142.
15. Ibid., 1:144, 148. The entire sermon appears in the section on Andrewes' life and preaching in my *Imagination Shaped: Old Testament Preaching in the Anglican Tradition* (Valley Forge, Pa.: Trinity Press International, 1995), 9–62.

Here, as always, Andrewes is looking for how the text touches us—indeed, how it reaches out to draw us in. In every sermon, Andrewes is setting forth the fundamental elements of Christian faith, but he knows that Christian doctrine has no life apart from human need. He never teaches about God in the abstract, about God apart from us. If God's incomparable majesty is the great theme that guides Calvin's reading of the Bible, for Andrewes it is the equally awesome depth of divine humility, in which our life is bound up inseparably with God's.

It has been said of Andrewes that he was "an important person not so much by what he did . . . and not so much even by what he wrote, as by what he was known to be."[16] Probably something similar can be said of every preacher. I listen to a preacher's message in light of what I know about her character, and accordingly, I take it more or less seriously. It is of course equally true that the message preached is one of the best clues to the preacher's personal character. Andrewes served as chaplain, preacher, and advisor to two monarchs[17] of the most powerful kingdom in Europe, as well as holding posts as Cambridge lecturer and college master, dean of Westminster, and bishop of the important see of Winchester. But what stands out in his preaching are the personal qualities—patience, humility, gentle firmness—that made him a beloved and memorable teacher of children (at the Westminster School, 1601–1605). He could teach about God's humility because every sermon bespeaks his own, reflected in the daily discipline of listening to Scripture and (as Russell Reno has defined humility) "lov[ing] that which God wishes us to hear."[18]

Confident though I am of his excellence, still I never assign Andrewes' sermons without wondering if it is asking too much of my students to stretch across four centuries in order to appreciate his peculiarly intense style, a style remarkable even in his own day. So I am always surprised anew when they repeatedly choose Andrewes above all others (including contemporary preachers) as a model for their own development as preachers. In this essay, I am trying to identify what it is about Andrewes' sermons that not only attracts but also instructs my students. Relying largely on their insights, I trace the ways in which a seventeenth-century preacher is found to be a trustworthy guide in addressing challenges encountered by preachers in the twenty-first century[19]—in some cases,

---

16. Alfred Barry, *Masters in English Theology* (New York: Dutton, 1877), 70.
17. Although Andrewes outlived James by eighteen months, ill health largely prevented him from court service during the succeeding reign of Charles I.
18. R. R. Reno, *In the Ruins of the Church* (Grand Rapids: Brazos, 2002), 180.
19. I am especially indebted to the unpublished thesis on Andrewes by Brent William Scott, "Essential Preaching" (master's thesis, Duke University Divinity School, 2002).

challenges we might otherwise have thought were unprecedented in Christian experience.

LOOKING AND MOVING

A few years ago a Navy chaplain enrolled in a seminar I was leading on preaching Isaiah, in which most of the assigned reading consisted of sermons. He had been given a year's study leave to do advanced work in preaching, and he was looking for a thesis topic. Six or seven weeks into the course, he said to me something like this: "I preach to eighteen- and nineteen-year-old recruits, and they are not going to sit still for 'three points and a poem.' I have about five minutes to make an impression on them. So far in my studies here, the one person who has grabbed my attention is Lancelot Andrewes. I'm convinced there is something to learn from his preaching that can be useful in working with my sailors."

Maybe this chaplain's congregation is an extreme example of what most North American and European preachers now face: listeners who are acculturated to speed and therefore to impatience. Moreover, *words* may be the thing with which they are least patient and (to be honest) least adept. On the whole, we are a culture of viewers rather than read- ers, as attested by statistics on the many hours Americans spend weekly in front of television sets, versus the scant minutes they spend reading. (Pollsters do not even register time spent reading the Bible or any serious theological literature.) On the face of it, it seems ridiculous to propose that in this situation we might learn something from a preacher who lived in one of the most word-conscious cultures of all time. In London, Andrewes preached to the most educated people of the day—and this was the generation of Shakespeare and Spenser.[20] Most of his preserved sermons were delivered at court, where for more than twenty years he addressed a king who styled himself, not just the titular Defender of the Faith, but a serious theologian.[21] Further, ecclesial affairs and their polit- ical ramifications had a place at the center of public life, a situation that seems drastically different from our own.

---

20. Andrewes and Edmund Spenser, author of *The Faerie Queene*, were both students at Pembroke Hall, Cambridge; their residence there overlapped for three years (1571–1574).

21. The long-standard picture of James as a bumbling amateur theologian has been fundamentally chal- lenged and revised in several recent studies (see, e.g., Kenneth Fincham, *Prelate as Pastor: The Episcopate of James I* [Oxford: Oxford University Press, 1990]; Linda Levy Peck, *The Mental World of the Jacobean Court* [Cambridge: Cambridge University Press, 1991]; Peter E. McCullough, *Sermons at Court: Politics and Reli- gion in Elizabethan and Jacobean Preaching* [Cambridge: Cambridge University Press, 1998]).

Yet perhaps there is one point of congruence. Andrewes makes an assumption with which many contemporary preachers could identify. He assumes that the people he addresses have come to church (or the chapel royal) without really knowing how to care about what is happening there. They take part in the great events in the corporate life of Christ—incarnation, the Lenten way of the cross, passion, crucifixion, resurrection, Pentecost[22]—and yet they do not know how to experience these as signal events in their own lives. Like many of us, Andrewes is speaking to people who have not willfully or even consciously turned away from God. They are simply distracted: busy, stimulated and overstimulated, balancing countless competing aspirations and obligations. They have never found or taken the time really to care about what God is doing in Jesus Christ. Instead of castigating his listeners as sinners, Andrewes speaks to them as people who do not see clearly what is happening before their eyes. Every sermon, then, has the dual goal of enabling Christians to *look* on God in Christ with true understanding and thus *be moved* to respond appropriately, with love and hope. It is a central conviction of early Anglican spirituality that we humans "have our part to play in our response to divine Love and in co-operation with grace."[23]

The central importance of seeing clearly may explain the most distinctive stylistic feature of Andrewes' rhetoric, namely, extreme economy of style. "No one is more master of the short sentence than Andrewes."[24] With respect to the comparative brevity of early Christian speech forms, Amos Wilder comments suggestively, "Persuasion may take a great deal of talk and argument, revelation does not."[25] If Andrewes' aim, like that of the evangelists, is to enable disciples to see Christ, then it is not surprising that he too creates a prose style that so often comes close to the rhythmic terseness of poetry. For poetry, as Goethe said, is *Schauen*, "looking."[26] Andrewes' sermons are therefore best read aloud. One experienced preacher reported that he could not make any headway with Andrewes until he started reading aloud on the train, where he found that the sound of the wheels helped him catch the rhythms. Although each of the court sermons was a full hour in length, they seem much

22. Most of Andrewes' court sermons were preached during Lent or on the most important days of the Christian year: Christmas, Ash Wednesday, Good Friday, Easter, Whitsun (Pentecost).

23. Martin Thornton, *English Spirituality: An Outline of Ascetical Theology according to the English Pastoral Tradition* (Cambridge, Mass.: Cowley, 1986), 302.

24. Eliot, "Lancelot Andrewes," 325.

25. Amos Wilder, *Early Christian Rhetoric: The Language of the Gospel* (Cambridge, Mass.: Harvard University Press, 1971), 21.

26. Ibid., 92.

shorter. Their effect is indeed like that of good poetry. What linger in the mind are a few words, indelibly impressed, and a sharp visual image conveyed by one line (and sometimes only a couple of words) of Scripture—although always that single image is shown to have multiple facets.[27] Moreover, it serves as a focal point for our reading of the whole gospel, the good news of God in Christ as understood through both Testaments.

Perhaps that kind of poetic preaching is just what can move this generation, in a culture more adept at reading images than words. In a recent call for "marketplace preaching," that is, a style of preaching that can reach people who are not already in the choir stalls, Calvin Miller asserts unequivocally, "Preaching is a matter of giving video hope. The video medium paints pictures that the audience is to absorb. . . . The only important question for the church is, Can the church become pictorially video in order to live, or will it remain only audio and die?"[28] His point is not that a sermon without accompanying video clip is a dead letter but rather that preachers must learn to think in images—indeed, in "moving pictures"—and "to transmit those images within the oral medium of the sermon. . . . Image communication may very well be the key to great preaching in the future."[29] Miller maintains that such a moving (in both senses) preaching style is fundamentally a matter of how we see. On this point, Andrewes and Miller are fully in agreement. Despite Miller's expressed concern that "the sermon shed its yesteryear image" and be done in "television words,"[30] I suggest that a preacher who precedes us by four centuries still has much to teach us about pictorial preaching. One thing we may learn from Andrewes is that there is more than one way for a preacher to be "pictorial."

"The Passion is a piece of perspective, and . . . we must set ourselves to see it if we will see it well."[31] The pictorial quality of Andrewes' preaching is especially evident in the three preserved Good Friday sermons. It is noteworthy that in each case, the particular words on which he "sets himself" in his preaching text point to some aspect of the act of seeing: "And they shall *look upon* me, whom they have pierced" (Zech. 12:10;

---

27. The depth of attention that Andrewes devotes to each word means that sometimes he does not finish treating even a single line, and so his court audience must wait a year or two for the continuation! In his Ash Wednesday sermon of 1621, he treats the first two words of Matt. 6:16, and then resumes a year later, assuming that the earlier points are still remembered! Similarly, some of the points outlined in his Christmas sermon of 1620 (on Matt. 2:1–2) are completed in his next Christmas sermon, of 1622. And beginning in 1620, he treats John 20:11–17 in three successive Easter sermons.
28. Calvin Miller, *Marketplace Preaching: How to Return the Sermon to Where It Belongs* (Grand Rapids: Baker, 1995), 39.
29. Ibid., 87–88.
30. Ibid., 37.
31. Andrewes, Good Friday 1605, 2:178.

1597); "*Consider, and behold,* if ever there were sorrow like my sorrow" (Lam. 1:12; 1604); "*Looking unto* Jesus the Author and Finisher of our faith" (Heb. 12:2; 1605). Repeatedly, he emphasizes that this is the day above all others for the office of preaching to clarify sight, so that Jesus Christ should be "visibly crucified among us."[32]

That emphasis itself bespeaks Andrewes' awareness of the culture of his own generation. In order to appreciate fully his artfulness as a preacher, it is well to remember the massive religious reorientation that occurred in England through a period that only slightly exceeded on either side the seventy years of his lifetime. Andrewes was born during the brief reign of Mary Tudor (1553–1558), so the early years of his life were spent in an environment of tremendous ecclesial and political flux. Following the Act of Supremacy (November 1534), which established Henry VIII as *summus episcopus,* head of both church and kingdom, the religious affiliation of the people changed with that of their sovereign. Officially at least, they were *English* Catholics until Henry's death in 1547; first moderate, then extreme Protestants under Edward VI (1547–1553); *Roman* Catholics under Mary; and again moderate Protestants, beginning with Elizabeth's long reign (1558–1603) and continuing under James (1603–1625). By the 1640s (about fifteen years after Andrewes' death), the Puritans were fiercely on the ascendancy, at least for a time.

Yet as Eamon Duffy has shown, the images and rituals of traditional Catholicism were firmly in place in English parish churches and in homes well into the 1540s and even beyond, inspiring the devotion of the vast majority of lay people. In other words, traditional religion did not slowly atrophy and die a more or less natural death in late medieval and early modern England. It was forcibly extinguished by deliberate actions of the monarchs, only intermitted during Mary's reign, until the job was completed in the last decades of the sixteenth century, about the time Andrewes went up to Cambridge (1571). Duffy notes the final, undramatic stage in "the passing of a world": "By 1573 the old priest [at Morebath], who had urged his flock on to set silver shoes on St Sidwell and lights before the Jesus altar, had come to see in the gift to his church of a handsome communion book and psalter for the new service a cause for prayerful rejoicing. In a thousand parishes in the 1570s and 1580s the same victory of reformed over traditional religion was silently and imperceptibly enacted."[33]

---

32. Andrewes, Good Friday 1597, 2:120; cf. Gal. 3:1.
33. Eamon Duffy, *The Stripping of the Altars: Traditional Religion in England c. 1400–c. 1580* (New Haven, Conn.: Yale University Press, 1992), 588.

The passion of Christ had constituted the imaginative center of the world of medieval Christianity. The events of Holy Week, from Palm Sunday to Easter, and especially those of Good Friday, were from year to year the most important public observances. And throughout the year, in every church, the crucifix and images of the passion were prominent reminders of its centrality. If "creeping to the cross" on Good Friday was the subject of frequent derision by the Reformers, that was doubtless because of the popularity of the practice. The passion was commemorated with considerable drama. The narrative from John's Gospel was read, and "at the words 'They parted my garments among them' the clerks parted and removed two linen cloths which had been specially placed for the purpose on the otherwise bare altar." Then a veiled crucifix was brought into the church and unveiled in three stages as the priest sang, each time on a higher note, "'Behold the wood of the cross, on which hung the saviour of the world. Come, let us worship.' Clergy and people then crept barefoot and on their knees to kiss the foot of the cross, held by two ministers."[34]

In stark contrast to the practice of previous generations of Christians in England, Andrewes and his congregation observed Good Friday in a chapel where there was no crucifix or any other visual memorial of the passion.[35] As a liturgical theologian with "high church" inclinations, he would have been (painfully) aware of what they were missing. Medieval Christianity as most people knew it provided religious nurturance in two forms: "a piety which seems rooted in stillness and looking"—at crucifix, stained glass, and images—and, conjoined with that, "a piety which seems geared to movement and elaborate communal celebration,"[36] such as processing with the cross, or creeping to it. Lancelot Andrewes' genius was to develop a style of preaching that sought to supply through words what was otherwise lacking in the religious experience of his hearers. In liturgically reduced circumstances, the verbal art of his sermons "Of the Passion" recreated for his hearers the twofold experience appropriate to this central day of the Christian year, first of *looking* long on the suffering Christ, and then of *moving* in humble response to what they saw.

The drama effected by words was Andrewes' antidote to what he saw as the great danger inherent in a narrowly Puritan piety, namely, that

---

34. Ibid., 29.
35. In 1621 a silver crucifix was reintroduced—after an absence of some sixty years—to Whitehall, the primary London chapel royal, in preparation for the visit of the Spanish Infanta, who was being courted as a wife for Prince Charles. See McCullough, *Sermons at Court*, 33–34, 201–3.
36. Duffy, *Stripping of the Altars*, 38.

faith could be understood in sterile intellectual terms,[37] as a matter merely of holding correct religious opinions, and conversion as "a turning of the brain only."[38] There is a remarkably contemporary ring to his repeated warning against letting our movement toward God be nothing more than a head trip: "Take heed of this error, as if repentance were a matter merely mental or intentional. It is not good notions in the brain, nor good motions in the mind will serve, these are but the sap within; look to the branches, what see you there? Look to *proferte*, what is brought forth."[39]

PASSION PERSPECTIVE

The superb Good Friday address of April 6, 1604—probably the first sermon Andrewes preached before James—is one of the best exemplars of his verbal art on any occasion.[40] He chose a text that had deep resonance with the traditional liturgy for the day: "Have ye no regard, O all ye that pass by the way? Consider, and behold, if ever there were sorrow like my sorrow" (Lam. 1:12). These are the opening words from the Improperia, the Reproaches from the Cross, which in the medieval church were sung in procession as the veiled crucifix was brought into the sanctuary.[41] Each of the brief poetic Reproaches contrasts the providential deliverance of God's people, manifested in the exodus and guidance through the wilderness, with "your" rejection of God, manifested in the torture and crucifixion of Christ.

A medieval preacher would have seen no need to defend a christological reading of the text from Lamentations. But Andrewes, sensitive to the Reformers' emphasis on the literal sense, regularly requires a hermeneutical warrant: "I demand then, 'Of whom speaketh the prophet[42] this? Of himself, or of some other?'" He supports his reading on two grounds: most fundamentally, the unvarying Christian practice, beginning with the Apostle Paul, of seeing the patriarchs and prophets as types of Christ.[43] But even a good theoretical argument makes for

---

37. See Peter Lake, "Lancelot Andrewes, John Buckeridge, and Avant-Garde Conformity at the Court of James I," in Peck, *Mental World of the Jacobean Court*, 113–33.

38. Andrewes, Ash Wednesday 1619, 1:363.

39. Andrewes, Ash Wednesday 1624, 1:439.

40. Although James was patron to many preachers, this was the first sermon to issue from the royal printing house, and the one most frequently reprinted during his reign. Six editions were printed before 1618 (McCullough, *Sermons at Court*, 150 n. 188). The sermon is reproduced in full, with annotations, on pages 103–27 of this volume.

41. Duffy, *Stripping of the Altars*, 29.

42. Andrewes accepts the traditional ascription of Lamentations to Jeremiah.

43. Andrewes, Good Friday 1604, 2:139–40.

unconvincing preaching. So, with the instinct of a master teacher, Andrewes shows also why that reading makes good *common* Christian sense: "None can say, neither Jeremy nor any other, *si fuerit dolor meus*,[44] as Christ can. No day of wrath like to his day, no sorrow to be compared to his—all are short of it—nor his to any; it exceedeth them all."[45]

The pathos sounded here is the keynote of the sermon, and its drama proceeds from the fact that throughout, the most important speaking voice is Christ's. Andrewes' words are no more than commentary that enables us to hear the poignancy of the question with which the Man on the cross confronts us. He actually begins his sermon mid-sentence, the words flowing without pause from the initial reading of the text:

> At the very reading or hearing of which verse there is none but will presently conceive it is the voice of a party in great extremity. In great extremity two ways: First, in such distress as never was any, "If ever there were sorrow like my sorrow." And then in that distress, having none to regard him, "Have ye no regard, all ye?"[46]

Although Andrewes is speaking from a pulpit elevated above the congregation (at eye level with the king's own elevated "closet"),[47] he consciously positions himself, along with everyone in the room, as part of the crowd milling about at the foot of the cross:

> Be it then to us (as to them it was, and as most properly it is) the speech of the Son of God, as this day hanging on the cross, to a sort of careless people that go up and down without any manner of regard of these his sorrows and sufferings, so worthy of all regard. "Have ye no regard? O all ye that pass by the way, consider and behold if ever there were sorrow like to my sorrow, which was done unto me, wherewith the Lord afflicted me in the day of the fierceness of his wrath."
>
> Here is a complaint, and here is a request. A complaint that we have not, a request that we would have the pains and passions of our Savior Christ in some regard. For first he complaineth, and

44. "If there were [any like] my sorrow."
45. Andrewes, Good Friday 1604, 2:139.
46. Ibid., 2:138.
47. See Peter McCullough's description of the architectural settings for court preaching (*Sermons at Court*, 11–49).

not without cause: "Have ye no regard?" And then, as willing to forget their former neglect (so they will yet do it), he falleth to entreat: "O consider and behold!"

"... If you considered as you should, you would regard as you ought."[48]

"The Passion is a piece of perspective."[49] It seems impossible that any preacher could lend a fresh perspective to our viewing of the cross. Yet Andrewes succeeds in bringing out a dimension of Christ's suffering we rarely (if ever) consider. The central insight of the sermon, derived from that leading question, is this: "[A]mong all the deadly sorrows of his most bitter passion, this, even this, seemeth to be his greatest of all and that which did most affect him: even the grief of the slender reckoning most men have it in."[50] Despite his interest in making the scene vivid, Andrewes avoids the trap of sensational preaching, dwelling excessively on Christ's physical suffering. Rather, he chooses a perspective that has more moral consequence for his hearers.

Focusing on our lack of regard, Andrewes shows that it is contrary to our nature and, further, illogical for us not to care more than we now do. Contrary to nature because this sorrow is unparalleled and "our nature is to regard things exceeding rare and strange"; so "be like yourselves in other things, and vouchsafe this, if not your chiefest, yet some regard."[51] Illogical because, moving beyond the grievous sorrow to investigate the even more important matter of its source, "we find it toucheth us near— and so near, so many ways, as we cannot choose but have some regard of it."[52] Summarily dismissing "Pilate and Caiaphas and the rest" as "instrumental causes only,"[53] Andrewes gives the verdict: "'Sin only is the murderer,' to say the truth, and our sins the murderers of the Son of God. . . . Which bringeth home this our text to us, even into our own bosoms, and applieth it most effectually to me that speak and to you that hear, to every one of us. And that with the prophet Nathan's application: *Tu es homo*, 'Thou art the man' (2 Sam. 12:7)—even thou, for whom God in 'his fierce wrath' thus afflicted him."[54]

48. Andrewes, Good Friday 1604, 2:140–41.
49. Andrewes, Good Friday 1605, 2:178.
50. Andrewes, Good Friday 1604, 2:155.
51. Ibid., 2:142–43.
52. Ibid., 2:149.
53. Andrewes similarly avoids anti-Semitism in his Good Friday sermon of 1597: "Ought not we much more justly and deservedly say of this piercing of Christ our Savior that we verily, even we, are the cause thereof, as verily we are, even the principals in this murder; and the Jews and others, on whom we seek to derive it, but only accessories and instrumental causes thereof" (2:127).
54. Andrewes, Good Friday 1604, 2:151.

Taking one more logical step, Andrewes discovers that even our own sin is not the final cause of this suffering. For the Son of God is not constrained to suffer by any external necessity, including the demand for justice. Finally, he suffers "for no other cause but 'because he would' (Isa. 53:7). . . . And why would he? No reason can be given but because he regarded us."[55] Turned in a new direction, that word we have heard now dozens of times suddenly acquires force. We are touched—at the same time convicted and moved—by the utter simplicity of Andrewes' affective logic. Having gained the decisive advantage, the preacher with gentle irony and steady repetition presses the point home: "For when he saw us a sort of forlorn sinners, *non prius natos quam damnatos,* 'damned as fast as born,' . . . even then in his love he regarded us, and so regarded us that he regarded not himself, to regard us."[56]

If we should persist in our unnatural and illogical lack of caring, the consequence will be tragic. What the medieval theologians called "the last things" always set the final horizon for Andrewes' preaching, yet they are never the focus. Christians are to live mindful of the realities of death and judgment, seen in passion perspective: "'And who regardeth the power of his wrath?' (Ps. 90:11). He that doth will surely regard this."[57] But Andrewes does not preach to terrify. Nor does he paint visions of heaven (and that marks a difference between his religious imagination and John Donne's). He stays close to the ground, working with the quiet assurance of a wise spiritual guide. Andrewes himself was far from being a beginner at the spiritual life; even with all his other responsibilities, he spent nearly five hours a day in prayer. Still, he did not forget what it is to begin. So he urges us immediately to make the modest commitment we can sustain, to render

> at leastwise some regard. Some, I say—the more the better, but in any wise some, and not as here no regard, none at all. Some ways to show we make account of it: to withdraw ourselves, to void our minds of other matters, to set this before us, to think upon it, to thank him for it, to regard him—and stay and see whether he will regard us or no. Sure he will, and we shall feel our "hearts pricked" with sorrow (Acts 2:37), by consideration of the cause in us—our sin—and again "warm within us" (Luke 24:32), by consideration of the cause in him—his love—till by

55. Ibid.
56. Ibid., 2:151–52.
57. Ibid., 2:155–56.

> some motion of grace he answer us, and show that our regard is accepted of him.[58]

Movement toward God is self-confirming. Although we may begin to move against our initial inclination, that disciplined effort gradually becomes genuine desire, as the divine reality becomes to us a felt reality, as we sense that in moving toward God we are coming into our own true nature.

Andrewes is, first and last, a practical theologian, not a speculative one. All his learning does not prevent him from seeing the people immediately before him and focusing on what they can understand; his own deep immersion in prayer does not cause him to overestimate what they can do today. The pattern in this sermon is typical of many others. Andrewes begins with a simple observation, drawn from the plain sense of the text and correlated with common human experience: of all human pains, the very sharpest is to know that no one cares that we suffer. He proceeds by means of rigorous logic, never deviating from the line of thought identified at the outset. Although he accurately exposes the illogic of how we often think and act, he never overreaches ordinary Christian common sense. He ends with an appeal to felt experience, and since it is his premise that we do not yet feel all that we should, he enables us to imagine what we may grow to feel, by the grace of God.

The language of the sermon itself bespeaks the thoroughly practical orientation of Andrewes' theology. Consciously and (doubtless, often) unconsciously, his words and phrases are informed by Scripture, by the liturgy, by the patristic theologians he knew so well. Still, the language is surprisingly everyday. Certainly Andrewes works with the Hebrew text, and with Greek and Latin translations, when the specificity of those languages seems to illumine a particular aspect of the text. But in choosing his own words, he prefers short Anglo-Saxon roots to long Latin ones,[59] and he is not afraid of punctuating his elegantly crafted sentences with occasional colloquialisms. So, for example, he describes the early church as "yet fresh and warm from Christ,"[60] and comments memorably on repentance, "the sooner the better because the more likely; the later the worse, because the less certain."[61] "The uncommon use of common language" is one of the marks of what Clayton Schmit calls "the hiddenness

---

58. Ibid., 2:156.
59. Joan Webber, "Celebration of Word and World in Lancelot Andrewes' Style," *Journal of English and Germanic Philology* 64 (1965): 258.
60. Andrewes, Ash Wednesday 1621, 1:392.
61. Andrewes, Ash Wednesday 1623, 1:431.

of excellence," the quality that enables preachers to deliver the gospel with power without themselves becoming the point of the sermon.[62] Andrewes has the skill and the humility to step out of the way and let the gospel as it is expressed in both Testaments make direct contact with the hearts of his hearers.

So what is it about Lancelot Andrewes that, after four hundred years, still makes him a helpful (for some, compelling) model for Christian preachers? In the end, I think it is the simplicity with which he reads Scripture—not intellectual simplicity, but the simplicity of conviction that enables him to read so intensively, "with an obedient attention born of believing that the words say exactly what we need to hear."[63] Watching him read, we may learn that hermeneutical discipline is, like every other healthy spiritual discipline, an indispensable way of drawing close to God. Of course, every member of the church does not practice every spiritual discipline. But in each congregation, someone must at all times be practicing every one that is essential. So if the church is indeed to fulfill its responsibility and prayer that the mind of its people be sound,[64] then its preachers must be practicing hermeneutics as a spiritual discipline.

Andrewes' own hermeneutical models were the theologian-preachers of the patristic period, among them Augustine, who makes the following observation on the prerequisite for understanding what we read: "The mind should be cleansed so that it is able to see that light [of truth] and cling to it once it is seen. Let us consider this cleansing to be as a journey or voyage home," to the God who "is our native country."[65] Augustine observes further: "But we do not come to Him who is everywhere present by moving from place to place, but by good endeavor and good habits." The caution against purposeless movement refers to the mind more than the body. Augustine and the other Fathers were in the habit of looking steadily, daily, deeply at the particular words of Scripture, "looking again and not elsewhere."[66] To look again and again at the words of

---

62. Clayton Schmit, *Too Deep for Words: A Theology of Liturgical Expression* (Louisville, Ky.: Westminster John Knox, 2002), 72. In his seminal study of New Testament rhetoric, Amos Wilder argues that the substance of the gospel is inseparable from the speech forms chosen by the early Christian writers, with their predilection for the vernacular and for common modes of discourse (*Early Christian Rhetoric*, 18, 39, 97, etc.).

63. Reno, *In the Ruins of the Church*, 185. Reno's chapter "Reflections in Aid of Theological Exegesis," and especially his treatment of hermeneutics as "the disciplines of attention that help us overcome [the] distance" between Scripture and ourselves, bears on my own thinking here (166).

64. See the prayer "For those who Influence Public Opinion" in the 1979 *Book of Common Prayer:*

Almighty God, you proclaim your truth in every age by many voices: Direct, in our time, we pray, those who speak where many listen and write what many read; that they may do their part in making the heart of this people wise, its mind sound, and its will righteous; to the honor of Jesus Christ our Lord. (*BCP*, 827)

65. Augustine, *On Christian Doctrine* 1.10–11, trans. D. W. Robertson Jr. (Indianapolis: Bobbs-Merrill, 1958), 13.
66. On "intensive reading" as a dominant practice of the patristic theologians, see Reno, *In the Ruins of the Church*, 176–78.

Scripture, with fascination and confidence that there is something we have not yet heard—that is the most important hermeneutical practice Andrewes learned from the Fathers, and the one we may learn from him. For our own generation in the church, when some preachers are so confident of their interpretations that their reading is often shallow, and others are without hope that Scripture can ever speak a sensible word to them, Lancelot Andrewes may be pointing the way home.

Lancelot Andrewes

A Sermon
preached before the King's Majesty, at Whitehall, on the sixth of April, A.D. MDCIV, being Good Friday[1]

Have ye no regard, O all ye that pass by the way? Consider, and behold, if ever there were sorrow like my sorrow, which was done unto me, wherewith the Lord did afflict me in the day of the fierceness of his wrath.

Lam. 1:12[2]

At the very reading or hearing of which verse there is none but will presently conceive it is the voice of a party in great extremity. In great extremity two ways: First, in such distress as never was any, "If ever there were sorrow like my sorrow." And then in that distress, having none to regard him, "Have ye no regard, all ye?"

To be afflicted, and so afflicted as none ever was, is very much. In that affliction, to find none to respect him or care for him, what can be more? In all our sufferings, it is a comfort to us that we have a *sicut*;[3] that nothing has befallen us but such as others have felt "the like" (1 Cor. 10:13). But here, *si fuerit sicut*, "if ever the like were"—that is, never the like was.

Again, in our greatest pains it is a kind of ease even to find some regard. Naturally we desire it, if we cannot be delivered, if we cannot be relieved, yet to be pitied (Job 19:21). It showeth there be yet some that are touched with the sense of our misery, that wish us well, and would give us ease if they could. But this afflicted here findeth not so much, neither the one nor the other, but is even as he were an

1. The basic text for the sermon comes from Lancelot Andrewes, *Ninety-Six Sermons*, ed. J. P. Wilson, 5 vols. (Oxford: J. H. Parker, 1841–1843; reprinted from the second edition, 1631), 2:138–57. As in the Donne sermon, the spelling and punctuation have been updated for the benefit of the modern "listener."

2. The texts that head Andrewes' sermons generally follow the Geneva Bible—the "Bible of the home" from the late sixteenth to the mid-seventeenth century. Scripture references are to the English versification (both Hebrew and English will be cited in the notes). Andrewes' quotations tend to be inexact; probably he is citing from memory. In all his sermons, he draws heavily on the Latin of Jerome's Vulgate. See J. P. Wilson, editor's preface to *Ninety-Six Sermons*, 1:v–viii, 2:vii; Gary DeMar, "The Geneva Bible: The Forgotten Translation," http://www.reformed.org/documents/geneva/Geneva.html.

3. From the Vulgate: *O vos omnes, qui transitis per viam, attendite et videte si est dolor sicut dolor meus: quoniam vindemiavit me ut locutus est Dominus in die irae furoris sui* (Lam. 1:12). *Sicut* is the Latin

outcast both of heaven and earth. Now verily an heavy case, and worthy to be put in this book of Lamentations.

I demand then, "Of whom speaketh the prophet this? Of himself, or of some other?"[4] This I find: there is not any of the ancient writers but do apply, yea in a manner appropriate, this speech to our Savior Christ. And that, this very day, the day of his passion, truly termed here the day of God's wrath, and wheresoever they treat of the passion, ever this verse cometh in. And to say the truth, to take the words strictly as they lie, they cannot agree or be verified of any but of him, and him only. For though some other, not unfitly, may be allowed to say the same words, it must be in a qualified sense; for in full and perfect propriety of speech, he and none but he. None can say, neither Jeremy nor any other, *si fuerit dolor meus*, as Christ can. No day of wrath like to his day, no sorrow to be compared to his—all are short of it—nor his to any; it exceedeth them all.

And yet, according to the letter, it cannot be denied but they be set down by Jeremy in the person of his own people, being then come to great misery, and of the holy city, then laid waste and desolate by the Chaldees. What then? *Ex Aegypto vocavi filium meum*, "Out of Egypt have I called my son" (Hos. 11:1), was literally spoken of this people too (Matt. 2:15), yet is by the evangelist applied to our Savior Christ. "My God, my God, why hast thou forsaken me?"—at the first uttered by David (Ps. 22:1). Yet the same words our Savior taketh himself (Matt. 27:46), and that more truly and properly than ever David could.

And of those of David's, and of these of Jeremy's, there is one and the same reason, of all which the ground is that correspondence which is between Christ and the patriarchs,

adverb that expresses comparability: "such as, just as, like." Andrewes makes this grammatical particle, which to most readers would seem unimportant, a touchstone for entering the text.

4. Cf. Acts 8:34.

prophets, and people before Christ—of whom
the apostle's rule is *omnia in figura continge-
bant illis* (1 Cor. 10:11),[5] that they were themselves types, and their sufferings, forerunning
figures of the great suffering of the Son of God.
Which maketh Isaac's offering, and Joseph's
selling, and Israel's calling from Egypt, and that
complaint of David's, and this of Jeremy's appli-
able to him, that he may take them to himself,
and the church ascribe them to him—and that
in more fitness of terms and more fullness of
truth than they were at the first spoken by
David, or Jeremy, or any of them all.

And this rule, and the steps of the Fathers[6]
proceeding by this rule, are to me a warrant to
expound and apply this verse, as they have done
before, to the present occasion of this time—
which requireth some such scripture to be considered by us as doth belong to his passion, who
this day poured out his most precious blood as
the only sufficient price of the dear purchase of
all our redemptions. Be it then to us (as to them
it was, and as most properly it is) the speech of
the Son of God, as this day hanging on the cross,
to a sort of careless people that go up and down
without any manner of regard of these his sorrows and sufferings, so worthy of all regard.
"Have ye no regard? O all ye that pass by the
way, consider and behold if ever there were sorrow like to my sorrow, which was done unto me,
wherewith the Lord afflicted me in the day of
the fierceness of his wrath."

Here is a complaint, and here is a request.[7] A
complaint that we have not, a request that we
would have the pains and passions of our Savior
Christ in some regard. For first he complaineth,
and not without cause: "Have ye no regard?"
And then, as willing to forget their former neglect (so they will yet do it), he falleth to entreat:
"O consider and behold!"

5. "All [these] came to them 'figurally.'"

6. Although Andrewes cites medieval theologians, the Church Fathers of the first six centuries are most seminal for his thought.

7. Having introduced the text and his warrant for applying it to Christ, Andrewes now sets forth the "division," the two major points of his sermon.

And what is that we should consider? The sorrow which he suffereth, and in it two things: the quality, and the cause. (1) The quality, *si fuerit sicut*, "if ever the like were," and that either in respect of *dolor* or *dolor meus*,[8] the sorrow suffered or the person suffering. (2) The cause, that is, God, that in his wrath, in his fierce wrath, doth all this to him—which cause will not leave us till it have led us to another cause in ourselves, and to another yet in him, all which serve to ripen us to regard.

These two then specially we are moved to regard. Regard is the main point. But because therefore we regard but faintly, because either we consider not, or not aright, we are called to consider seriously of them. As if he should say, "Regard you not? If you did consider, you would. If you considered as you should, you would regard as you ought." Certainly the passion, if it were throughly[9] considered, would be duly regarded. Consider then.

So the points are two: (1) the quality, and (2) the cause of his suffering. And the duties two: to consider, and regard; so to consider that we regard them, and him for them.[10]

PART I—THE QUALITY OF THE SORROW

"Have ye no regard, etc.?"[11] To ease this complaint and to grant this request, we are to regard. And that we may regard, we are to consider the pains of his passion—which, that we may reckon no easy common matter of light moment, to do or not to do as we list,[12] first, a general stay is made of all passengers this day. For, as it were, from his cross doth our Savior address this his speech to them that go to and fro the day of his passion, without so much as entertaining a thought or vouchsafing a look that way. *O vos qui transitis!* "O you that pass

8. "sorrow" or "my sorrow."

9. throughly—thoroughly.

10. The *exordium* (the introduction to a formal sermon generally employed by seventeenth-century preachers) typically concludes by outlining the argument of the whole sermon.

11. It is impossible to know how much of the verse Andrewes would have repeated at this point.

12. list—wish.

by the way," stay and consider. To them frameth he his speech, that pass by; to them, and to them all: *O vos omnes qui transitis,* "O all ye that pass by the way, stay and consider."

Which very stay of his showeth it to be some important matter, in that it is of *all.* For as for some to be stayed, and those the greater some, there may be reason. The most part of those that go thus to and fro may well intend[13] it; they have little else to do. But to except none, not some special person, is hard. What know we their haste? Their occasions may be such, and so urgent, as they cannot stay.[14] Well, what haste, what business soever, pass not by; stay though. As much to say as, be they never so great, your occasions—they are not, they cannot be so great as this. How urgent soever, this is more, and more to be intended. The regard of this is worthy the staying of a journey. It is worth the considering of those that have never so great affairs in hand. So material is this sight in his account, which serveth to show the exigence[15] of this duty. But as for this point, it needeth not be stood upon[16] to us here at this time. We are not going by; we need not be stayed; we have stayed all other our affairs to come hither. And here we are all present before God, to have it set before us, that we may consider it. Thither then let us come.

That which we are called to behold and consider is his sorrow. And sorrow is a thing which of itself nature inclineth us to behold, "as being ourselves in the body" (Heb. 13:3), which may be one day in the like sorrowful case. Therefore will every good eye turn itself and look upon them that lie in distress. Those two in the Gospel that passed by the wounded man— before they passed by him, though they helped him not as the Samaritan did, yet they *looked upon* him as he lay (Luke 10:32). But this party

13. intend—direct the eyes or mind toward.

14. Here Andrewes subtly alludes to how some "special persons" in his court audience would be thinking, although within a few sentences he commends his listeners for what they have done well, namely, put aside their "great affairs" to come to chapel that day.

15. exigence—urgency.

16. stood upon—belabored, dwelt upon.

here lieth not. He is lift up as the serpent in the wilderness (John 3:14),[17] that unless we turn our eyes away purposely, we can neither will nor choose but behold him.

But because to behold and not to consider is but to gaze, and gazing the angel blameth in the apostles themselves (Acts 1:11), we must do both. Both "behold" and "consider": look *upon* with the eye of the body (that is, "behold"), and look *into* with the eye of the mind (that is, "consider"). So saith the prophet here. And the very same doth the apostle advise us to do: first ἀφορᾶν, to look upon him, that is, to "behold"; and then ἀναλογίζεσθαι, to think upon him, that is, to "consider" his sorrow (Heb. 12:2[–3]).[18] Sorrow sure would be considered.

18. "*Looking unto* Jesus the author and finisher of our faith . . . , *consider* therefore him who endured such" (Heb. 12:2–3 GB; traditionally ascribed to "the apostle" Paul). This was the text for Andrewes' Good Friday sermon the following year, 1605.

Now then, because as the quality of the sorrow is, accordingly it would be considered—for if it be but a common sorrow, the less will serve, but if it be some special, some very heavy case, the more would be allowed it, for proportionably with the suffering, the consideration is to arise—to raise our consideration to the full, and to elevate it to the highest point, there is upon his sorrow set a *si fuerit sicut*, a note of highest eminency.[19] For *si fuerit sicut* are words that have life in them and are able to quicken our consideration, if it be not quite dead. For by them we are provoked, as it were, to "consider," and considering, to see whether ever any *sicut* may be found to set by it,[20] whether ever any like it. For if never any . . . Our nature is to regard things exceeding rare and strange, and such as the like whereof is not else to be seen. Upon this point then, there is a case made, as if he should say, "If ever the like, regard not this. But if never any, be like yourselves in other things, and vouchsafe this, if not your chiefest, yet some regard."

19. *Si fuerit sicut* introduces a hypothetical statement: "if there were any like . . ." As Andrewes emphasizes, the hypothesis of incomparability is a rhetorical device that naturally awakens interest.

20. set by it—compare with it.

The Suffering

To enter this comparison, and to show it for such—that are we to do, three sundry ways. For three sundry ways, in three sundry words, are these sufferings of his here expressed, all three within the compass of the verse:

The first is מכאוב, *Mac-ob*, which we read "sorrow," taken from a wound or stripe, as all do agree.

The second is עולל, *Gholel*; we read "done to me," taken from a word that signifieth melting in a furnace (as St. Hierome noteth out of the Chaldee,[21] who so translateth it).

The third is הוגה, *Hoga*, where we read "afflicted," from a word which importeth renting off, or bereaving. The old Latin turneth it *vindemiavit me*, as a vine whose fruit is all plucked off. The Greek, with Theodoret, ἀπεφύλλισέ με,[22] as a vine or tree whose leaves are all beaten off, and is left naked and bare.

In these three are comprised his sufferings: wounded, melted, and bereft leaf and fruit—that is, all manner of comfort. Of all that is penal, or can be suffered, the common division is *sensus et damni*, grief for that we feel, or for that we forgo.[23] For that we feel in the two former: wounded in body, melted in soul; for that we forgo in the last: bereft all, left neither fruit nor so much as a leaf to hang on him. According to these three, to consider his sufferings, and to begin first with the first: the pains of his body, his wounds and his stripes.

Our very eye will soon tell us no place was left in his body where he might be smitten and was not. His skin and flesh rent with the whips and scourges, his hands and feet wounded with the nails, his head with the thorns, his very heart with the spear point; all his senses, all his

21. He refers to Jerome's consultation of the Targum, the (sometimes paraphrastic) Aramaic translation of the Hebrew Scriptures. By modern conventions, the word עולל is pronounced *'ôlal*.

22. Citing Theodoret's fifth-century commentary on Lamentations, which reads ἐπεφύλλισέ με (PG 81·783–84),

23. Andrewes is using legal terminology. *Poena sensus* denotes the infliction of corporal punishment; *poena damni*, the pain of loss or deprivation, e.g., a monetary fine.

parts laden with whatsoever wit or malice could invent. His blessed body given as an anvil to be beaten upon with the violent hands of those barbarous miscreants, till they brought him into this case of *si fuerit sicut.* For Pilate's *Ecce homo!*[24] (John 19:5), his showing him with an *Ecce*, as if he should say, "Behold, look if ever you saw the like rueful spectacle"—this very showing of his showeth plainly he was then come into woeful plight. So woeful as Pilate verily believed his very sight so pitiful as it would have moved the hardest heart of them all to have relented and said, "This is enough; we desire no more." And this for the wounds of his body, for on this we stand not.

In this one, peradventure some *sicut* may be found, in the pains of the body. But in the second, the sorrow of the soul, I am sure, none. And indeed, the pain of the body is but the body of pain; the very soul of sorrow and pain is the soul's sorrow and pain. "Give me any grief save the grief of the mind," saith the wise man; for, saith Solomon, "The spirit of a man will sustain all his other infirmities, but a wounded spirit, who can bear?" (Prov. 18:14). And of this, this of his soul, I dare make a case, *si fuerit sicut.*

"He began to be troubled in soul," saith St. John (12:27); "to be in an agony," saith St. Luke (22:44); "to be in anguish of mind and deep distress," saith St. Mark (14:33). To have his soul round about on every side environed with sorrow, and that sorrow to the death (Matt. 26:38). Here is trouble, anguish, agony, sorrow, and deadly sorrow. But it must be such as never the like: so it was, too. The estimate whereof we may take from the second word of melting, that is, from his sweat in the garden (Luke 22:44): strange, and the like whereof was never heard or seen. No manner violence offered him in body, no man touching him or being near

24. "Behold the man!"

him; in a cold night (for they were fain[25] to have a fire within doors), lying abroad in the air and upon the cold earth—to be all of a sweat, and that sweat to be blood; and not as they call it *diaphoreticus*, "a thin, faint sweat," but *grumosus*, "of great drops"; and those so many, so plenteous, as they went through his apparel and all, and through all streamed to the ground, and that in great abundance—read, inquire, and consider, *si fuerit sudor sicut sudor iste*; "if ever there were sweat like this sweat of his." Never the like sweat certainly, and therefore never the like sorrow.

Our translation is "done unto me," but we said the word properly signifieth (and so St. Hierome and the Chaldee paraphrast read it) "melted me." And truly it should seem, by this fearful sweat of his, he was near some furnace, the feeling whereof was able to cast him into that sweat, and to turn his sweat into drops of blood. And sure it was so. For see, even in the very next words of all to this verse, he complaineth of it: *Ignem misit in ossibus meis*,[26] that a fire was sent into his bones (Lam. 1:13), which melted him and made that bloody sweat to distill from him. That hour, what his feelings were, it is dangerous to define; we know them not, we may be too bold to determine of them. To very good purpose it was that the ancient fathers of the Greek Church in their liturgy, after they have recounted all the particular pains as they are set down in his passion, and by all and by every one of them called for mercy, do after all shut up all with this: Δι ἀγνωστῶν κόπων καὶ βασάνων ἐλέησον καὶ σῶσον ἡμᾶς, "By thine unknown sorrows and sufferings, felt by thee, but not distinctly known by us, have mercy upon us, and save us!" Now, though this suffice not—nothing near—yet let it suffice, the time being short for his pains of body and soul.

25. fain—obliged, content.

26. "He sent fire into my bones."

For those of the body, it may be some may have endured the like, but the sorrows of his soul are "unknown sorrows." And for them none ever have, ever have or ever shall suffer the like; the like, or near the like in any degree.

And now to the third. It was said before, to be in distress—such distress as this was—and to find none to comfort—nay, not so much as to regard him—is all that can be said to make his sorrow a *non sicut*.[27] Comfort is it by which, in the midst of all our sorrows, we are *confortati*, that is, strengthened and made the better able to bear them all out. And who is there, even the poorest creature among us, but in some degree findeth some comfort or some regard at somebody's hands? For if that be not left, the state of that party is here in the third word said to be like the tree whose leaves and whose fruit are all beaten off quite, and itself left bare and naked both of the one and of the other.

And such was our Savior's case in these his sorrows this day, and that so as what is left the meanest[28] of the sons of men, was not left him, not a leaf. Not a leaf! "Leaves" I may well call all human comforts and regards, whereof he was then left clean desolate. "His own" [John 1:11]—they among whom he had gone about all his life long, healing them, teaching them, feeding them, doing them all the good he could—it is they that cry, "Not him, no, but Barabbas rather!" (John 18:40); "Away with him!" (John 19:15); "His blood be upon us and our children!" (Matt. 27:25). It is they that in the midst of his sorrows shake their head at him and cry, "Ah, thou wretch!"; they that in his most disconsolate estate cry, "Eli, Eli," in most barbarous manner deride him and say, "Stay, and you shall see Elias come presently and take him down" (Mark 15:29, [34–]36). And this was their regard. But these were but withered

27. "[there is] nothing like," i.e., something beyond compare.

28. meanest—poorest.

leaves. They then that on earth were nearest him of all, the greenest leaves and likest to hang on and to give him some shade—even of them, some bought and sold him, others denied and forswore him, but all fell away and forsook him. Ἀπεφύλλισέ με, saith Theodoret: not a leaf left.

But leaves are but leaves, and so are all earthly stays. The fruit then, the true fruit of the Vine, indeed, the true comfort in all heaviness, is *desuper* ("from above")[29]—is divine consolation. But *vindemiavit me,* saith the Latin text—even that was, in this his sorrow this day, bereft[30] him too. And that was his most sorrowful complaint of all others: not that his friends upon earth but that his Father from heaven had forsaken him; that neither heaven nor earth yielded him any regard, but that between the passioned powers of his soul and whatsoever might any ways refresh him there was a traverse[31] drawn, and he left in the state of a weather-beaten tree, all desolate and forlorn. Evident, too evident, by that his most dreadful cry, which at once moved all the powers in heaven and earth: "My God, my God, why hast thou forsaken me?" (Matt. 27:46).[32] Weigh well that cry. Consider it well and tell me *si fuerit clamor sicut clamor iste,* "if ever there were cry like that of his." Never the like cry, and therefore never the like sorrow.

It is strange, very strange, that of none of the martyrs the like can be read, who yet endured most exquisite pains in their martyrdoms. Yet we see with what courage, with what cheerfulness, how even singing, they are reported to have passed through their torments. Will ye know the reason? St. Augustine setteth it down: *Martyres non eripuit, sed nunquid deseruit?* "He delivered not his martyrs, but did he forsake them?" He delivered not their bodies, but he forsook not their souls but

29. Cf. Jas. 1:17: "Every good giving, and every perfect gift is from above, and cometh down from the Father of lights" (GB).

30. bereft—here, taken from him violently.

31. traverse—impediment.

32. Cf. Ps. 22:2 [1 Eng.].

distilled into them the dew of his heavenly comfort, an abundant supply for all they could endure. Not so here. *Vindemiavit me*, saith the prophet; *Dereliquisti me*,[33] saith he himself— no comfort, no supply at all.

Leo it is that first said it,[34] and all antiquity allow[35] of it, *Non solvit unionem, sed subtraxit visionem*, "The union was not dissolved, true; but the beams, the influence was restrained." And for any comfort from thence his soul was even as a scorched heath-ground, without so much as any drop of dew of divine comfort. As a naked tree: no fruit to refresh him within, no leaf to give him shadow without. The power of darkness let loose to afflict him, the influence of comfort restrained to relieve him. It is a *non sicut*, this; it cannot be expressed as it should and as other things may. In silence we may admire it, but all our words will not reach it. And though to draw it so far as some do is little better than blasphemy, yet on the other side to shrink it so short as other some do cannot be but with derogation to his love—who, to kindle our love and loving regard, would come to a *non sicut* in his suffering. For so it was, and so we must allow it to be. This, in respect of his passion, *dolor*.

The Person

Now in respect of his person, *dolor meus*. Whereof, if it please you to take a view even of the person thus wounded, thus afflicted and forsaken, you shall then have a perfect *non sicut*. And indeed the person is here a weighty circumstance;[36] it is thrice repeated—*meus, mihi, me*[37]—and we may not leave it out. For as is the person, so is the passion;[38] and any one, even the very least degree of wrong or disgrace offered to a person of excellency is more than a hundred times more [than] to one of mean condition, so weighty is the circumstance of the

33. "You have abandoned me" (citing the cry from the cross).

34. Leo the Great, *On the Passion of the Lord* 17.1–2 (PL 54:373).

35. allow—acknowledge.

36. a weighty circumstance—of great importance.

37. "mine, to me, me."

38. Here, as often in the sermon, "passion" designates suffering in general, and not only Christ's suffering on the cross.

person. Consider then how great the person was, and I rest fully assured here we boldly challenge and say, *"Si fuerit sicut!"*

Ecce homo! saith Pilate first (John 19:5); a man he is as we are. And were he but a man, nay, were he not a man but some poor drab[39] creature, it were great ruth[40] to see him so handled as he was.

"A man," saith Pilate, and a "just man," saith Pilate's wife. "Have thou nothing to do with that just man" (Matt. 27:19). And that is one degree farther. For though we pity the punishment even of malefactors themselves, yet ever most compassion we have of them that suffer and be innocent. And he was innocent; Pilate and Herod (Luke 23:14–15) and "the prince of this world" (John 14:30), his very enemies, being his judges.

Now among the innocent, the more noble the person, the more heavy the spectacle. And never do our bowels[41] yearn so much as over such. "Alas, alas for that noble prince," saith this prophet (Jer. 22:18),[42] the style of mourning for the death of a great personage. And he that suffered here is such: even a principal person among the sons of men, of the race royal, descended from kings. Pilate styled him so in his title, and he would not alter it (John 19:[19–]22).

Three degrees. But yet we are not at our true *quantus*.[43] For he is yet more, more than the highest of the sons of men, for he is the Son of the Most High God. Pilate saw no farther but *Ecce homo!* (John 19:5). The centurion did: *Vere Filius Dei erat hic,* "Now truly this was the Son of God" (Mark 15:39). And here all words forsake us, and every tongue becometh speechless.

We have no way to express it but *a minore ad majus*.[44] Thus of this book, the book of Lamentations, one special occasion was the death of King Josias, but "Behold, a greater than Josias is

39. drab—dispirited.

40. ruth—pity, sorrow.

41. Andrewes and other seventeenth-century English speakers followed the biblical writers in referring to the bowels as the seat of compassion.

42. Andrewes regards Jeremiah as author of Lamentations as well as of the book that bears his name.

43. The Latin adjective *quantus* designates a measure of size, importance, or (in this case) degree: "how great." Andrewes is building by degrees a "quantitative" argument to prove the proposition stated above, that wrong done to a great person is (one hundred times!) more serious than to an ordinary person.

44. A term of logic: "from smaller to greater."

here."[45] Of King Josias, as a special reason of mourning, the prophet saith, *spiritus oris nostri, christus Domini,* "the very breath of our nostrils, the Lord's anointed" (Lam. 4:20) (for so are all good kings in their subjects' accounts);[46] he is gone. But behold, here is not *christus Domini* but *Christus Dominus,* "the Lord's christ" but the "Lord Christ himself" [Luke 2:11][47]—and that not coming to an honorable death in battle as Josias did but to a most vile reproachful death, the death of malefactors in the highest degree. And not slain outright as Josias was but mangled and massacred in most pitiful strange manner: wounded in body, wounded in spirit, left utterly desolate. O consider this well, and confess the case is truly put, *si fuerit dolor sicut dolor meus!* Never, never the like person; and if as the person is, the passion be, never the like passion to his.

It is truly affirmed that any one, even the least drop of blood, even the least pain, yea of the body only, of this so great a person, any *dolor* with this *meus* had been enough to make a *non sicut* of it. That is enough, but that is not all. For add now the three other degrees; add to this person those wounds, that sweat, and that cry, and put all together, and I make no manner question the like was not, shall not, cannot ever be. It is far above all that ever was or can be; *abyssus est.*[48] Men may drowsily hear it and coldly affect[49] it, but principalities and powers stand abashed at it. And for the quality both of the passion and of the person, that never the like, thus much.

PART II—THE CAUSE

Now to proceed to the cause and to consider it, for without it we shall have but half a regard, and scarce that. Indeed, set the cause aside, and the passion—as rare as it is—is yet but a dull

45. Cf. Matt. 12:41–42; Luke 11:31–32.

46. This aside reflects Andrewes' genuine (theological) conviction of "the divine right of kings."

47. Andrewes plays on two uses of the word *christus:* as a common noun ("anointed one") and as the designation of Jesus as Messiah, above all others the anointed of God.

48. "It is hell."

49. affect—feel, respond to.

and heavy sight. We list[50] not much look upon spectacles of that kind. Though never so strange, they fill us full of pensive thoughts and make us melancholic. And so doth this, till upon examination of the cause we find it toucheth us near—and so near, so many ways, as we cannot choose but have some regard of it.

What was done to him we see. Let there now be a quest of inquiry to find who was doer of it. Who? Who but the "power of darkness" (Luke 22:53): wicked Pilate, bloody Caiaphas, the envious priests, the barbarous soldiers? None of these are returned[51] here. We are too low by a great deal if we think to find it among men. *Quae fecit mihi Deus*[52]—it was God that did it. An hour of that day was the hour of the "power of darkness"; but the whole day itself, is said here plainly, was the day of the wrath of God. God was a doer in it: "wherewith God hath afflicted me."

God afflicteth some in mercy, and others in wrath. This was in his wrath. In his wrath God is not alike to all; some he afflicteth in his more gentle and mild, others in his fierce wrath. This was in the very fierceness of his wrath; his sufferings, his sweat, and cry show as much. They could not come but from a wrath *si fuerit sicut*, for we are not past *non sicut*—no, not here. In this part it followeth us still, and will not leave us in any point, not to the end.

The cause then in God was wrath. What caused this wrath? God is not wroth but with sin, nor grievously wroth but with grievous sin. And in Christ there was no grievous sin—nay, no sin at all. God did it; the text is plain. And in his fierce wrath he did it. For what cause? For God forbid God should do as did Annas the high priest: cause him to be smitten without cause (John 18:22)! "God forbid," saith Abraham, "the Judge of the world" should do

50. list—like (to).

51. In this context, "returned" is a legal term for rendering a verdict or the results of an investigation.
52. ". . . which God did to me." The phrase does not appear in the Vulgate, but it is an accurate Latin rendering of the Hebrew.

wrong to any (Gen. 18:25)! To any, but specially to his own Son, that his Son, of whom with thundering voice from heaven he testifieth, all his joy and delight were in him, in him only he was "well pleased" [Matt. 3:17]. And how then could his wrath wax hot to do all this unto him?

There is no way to preserve God's justice and Christ's innocency both but to say as the angel said of him to the prophet Daniel, "The Messias shall be slain," וְאֵין לוֹ (ve-en-lo), "shall be slain, but not for himself" (Dan. 9:26).[53] "Not for himself"? For whom then? For some others. He took upon him the person of others, and so doing, justice may have her course and proceed. Pity it is to see a man pay that he never took. But if he will become a surety, if he will take on him the person of the debtor, so he must. Pity to see a silly[54] poor lamb lie bleeding to death. But if it must be a sacrifice (such is the nature of a sacrifice), so it must. And so Christ, though without sin in himself, yet as a surety, as a sacrifice, may justly suffer for others, if he will take upon him their persons. And so God may justly give way to his wrath against him.

And who be those others? The prophet Esay telleth us, and telleth it us seven times over for failing:[55]

53. The phrase is difficult in Hebrew and may involve corruption. The whole clause may also be translated, "One who is anointed shall be cut off and have nothing."

54. silly—defenseless; a conventional (poetic) epithet of sheep.

55. failing—generally, weakness; here, lack of attention.

He took upon him our infirmities,
and bare our maladies.
He was wounded for our iniquities,
and broken for our transgressions.
The chastisement of our peace was upon
    him,
and with his stripes were we healed.
All we as sheep were gone astray,
and turned every man to his own way;
and the Lord hath laid upon him
the iniquity of us *all*.

(Isa. 53:4–6)

"All . . . , all": even those that pass to and fro, and for all this regard neither him nor his passion.

The short is, it was we that for our sins, our many great and grievous sins—*si fuerit sicut,* the like whereof never were—should have sweated this sweat and have cried this cry; should have been smitten with these sorrows by the fierce wrath of God, had not he stepped between the blow and us and latched it in his own body and soul, even the dint of the fierceness of the wrath of God. O the *non sicut* of our sins, that could not otherwise be answered!

To return then a true verdict: it is we—we, wretched sinners that we are—that are to be found the principals in this act, and those on whom we seek to shift it, to drive it from ourselves—Pilate and Caiaphas and the rest—but instrumental causes only.[56] And it is not the executioner that killeth the man properly (that is, they); no, nor the judge, which is God in this case; only sin. *Solum peccatum homicida est,* "Sin only is the murderer," to say the truth, and our sins the murderers of the Son of God, and the *non sicut* of them the true cause of the *non sicut* both of God's wrath and of his sorrowful sufferings. Which bringeth home this our text to us, even into our own bosoms, and applieth it most effectually to me that speak and to you that hear, to every one of us.[57] And that with the prophet Nathan's application: *Tu es homo,* "Thou art the man" (2 Sam. 12:7)—even thou, for whom God "in his fierce wrath" thus afflicted him. Sin then was the cause on our part, why we, or some other for us.

But yet what was the cause, why he on his part? What was that that moved him thus to become our surety and to take upon him our debt and danger, that moved him thus to lay upon his soul a sacrifice for our sin? Sure, *oblatus est quia voluit,* saith Esay again, "offered he

56. In his Good Friday sermons, Andrewes consistently refuses to follow the practice, standard among Christian preachers from antiquity through the Middle Ages, of placing primary blame for the crucifixion on the Jews. On this important point, he might be compared favorably to many modern preachers.

57. The emphasis on applying the text to ourselves in a personal (yet not private) way is one of the hallmarks of early Anglican preaching (in contrast to the Puritan preference for straight line-by-line exposition) and may be its distinctive contribution to the development of Christian preaching. See Ellen F. Davis, *Imagination Shaped: Old Testament Preaching in the Anglican Tradition* (Valley Forge, Pa.: Trinity Press International, 1995), 6–7.

was" for no other cause but "because he would" (Isa. 53:7).[58] For unless he would, he needed not. Needed not for any necessity of justice (for no lamb was ever more innocent), nor for any necessity of constraint (for "twelve legions of angels" [Matt. 26:53] were ready at his command), but because he would.

And why would he? No reason can be given but because he regarded us—mark that reason. And what were we? Verily, utterly unworthy even his least regard, not worth the taking up, not worth the looking after. *Cum inimici essemus*, saith the apostle, "we were his enemies" (Rom. 5:[10]) when he did it—without all desert[59] before and without all regard after he had done and suffered all this for us. And yet he would regard us that so little regard him. For when he saw us a sort of forlorn sinners, *non prius natos quam damnatos*, "damned as fast as born," as being "by nature children of wrath" (Eph. 2:3), and yet still "heaping up wrath against the day of wrath" (Rom. 2:5) by the errors of our life, till the time of our passing hence; and then the "fierce wrath of God" ready to overwhelm us, and to make us endure the terror and torments of a never-dying death, another *non sicut* yet. When, I say, he was in this case, he was moved with compassion over us and undertook all this for us. Even then in his love he regarded us, and so regarded us that he regarded not himself, to regard us. Bernard saith most truly: *Dilexisti me, Domine, magis quam te, quando mori voluisti pro me;*[60] in suffering all this for us thou showedst, Lord, that we were more dear to thee, that thou regardest us more than thine own self. And shall this regard find no regard at our hands?

It was sin then, and the heinousness of sin in us, that provoked wrath, and the fierceness of his wrath, in God. It was love, and the greatness

58. He cites the Vulgate. The Hebrew might mean either "he was afflicted" or "he humbled/submitted himself."

59. desert—deserving.

60. "You have chosen me, Lord, over yourself, in as much as you wished to die for me." The citation is in fact from Augustine, *Soliloquiorum animae ad Deum* 1.13 (PL 40:874). Andrewes correctly cites Augustine in his Lenten sermon preached on April 4, 1596, on 2 Cor. 12:15.

of his love in Christ, that caused him to suffer the sorrows, and the grievousness of these sorrows—and all for our sakes.

And indeed, but only to testify the *non sicut* of this his love, all this needed not that was done to him. One, any one, even the very least of all the pains he endured, had been enough— enough in respect of the *meus*, enough in respect of the *non sicut* of his person. For that which setteth the high price on this sacrifice is this: that he which offereth it unto God is God. But if little had been suffered, little would the love have been thought that suffered so little, and as little regard would have been had of it. To awake our regard then—or to leave us excuseless, if we continue regardless—all this he bare for us, that he might as truly make a case of *si fuerit amor sicut amor meus* as he did before of *si fuerit dolor sicut dolor meus*.[61] We say we will regard love. If we will, here it is to regard.

61. "If there were any love like my love"; "if there were any sorrow like my sorrow."

PART III—THE BENEFIT

So have we the causes, all three: wrath in God, sin in ourselves, love in him. Yet have we not all we should. For what of all this? What good? *Cui bono?*[62] That—that is it indeed that we will regard, if anything, as being matter of benefit, the only thing in a manner the world regardeth, which bringeth us about to the very first words again. For the very first words which we read, "Have ye no regard?" are in the original לוֹא אֲלֵיכֶם, *lo alechem*, which the Seventy[63] turn, word for word, οὐ πρὸς ὑμᾶς; and the Latin, likewise: *Nonne ad vos pertinet?* "Pertains it not to you"—that you regard it no better? For these two, pertaining and regarding, are folded one in another and go together so commonly as one is taken often for the other. Then to be sure to

62. *Cui bono* ("for whose good") is the legal principle that the person who *benefits* from a crime is probably the one who committed it. This is precisely Andrewes' argument about our responsibility for the crucifixion.

63. "The Seventy" refers to the Septuagint (LXX), the Greek translation of the Hebrew Scriptures; according to tradition, seventy ancient translators, each working in isolation, miraculously produced seventy identical translations.

bring us to regard, he urgeth this: "Pertains not all this to you?" Is it not for your good? Is not the benefit yours? Matters of benefit, they pertain to you, and without them, love and all the rest may pertain to whom they will.[64]

Consider then the inestimable benefit that groweth unto you from this incomparable love. It is not impertinent[65] this, even this: that to us hereby all is turned about clean contrary—that "by his stripes we are healed," by his sweat we refreshed, by his forsaking we received to grace. That this day, to him the day of the fierceness of God's wrath, is to us the day of the fullness of God's favor, as the apostle calleth it, "a day of salvation" (2 Cor. 6:2). In respect of that he suffered (I deny not), an evil day, a day of heaviness. But in respect of that which he by it hath obtained for us, it is as we truly call it a Good day, a day of joy and jubilee. For it doth not only rid us of that wrath which pertaineth to us for our sins, but farther, it maketh that pertain to us whereto we had no manner of right at all.

For not only by his death as by the death of our sacrifice, by the blood of his cross as by the blood of the Paschal Lamb, the Destroyer passeth over us and we shall not perish (Exod. 12:13), but also by his death as by the death of our High Priest—for he is priest and sacrifice both (Num. 35:25)[66]—we are restored from our exile, even to our former forfeited estate in the land of promise. Or rather, as the apostle saith, *non sicut delictum sic donum*[67] (Rom. 5:15), not to the same estate but to one nothing like it— that is, one far better than the estate our sins bereft us. For they deprived us of paradise, a place on earth. But by the purchase of his blood we are entitled to a far higher, even the kingdom of heaven, and his blood, not only the blood of "remission," to acquit us of our sins,

64. Andrewes' resolutely practical orientation evidences itself in the fact that his sermons rarely end without asking, "So what? What difference does it make for me?"

65. impertinent—irrelevant.

66. Cf. Heb. 4:14–5:10.

67. "The gift is not like the trespass."

but "the blood of the Testament" too (Matt. 26:28), to bequeath us and give us estate in that heavenly inheritance.

Now whatsoever else, this I am sure is a *non sicut*, as that which the eye by all it can see, the ear by all it can hear, the heart by all it can conceive cannot pattern it or set the like by it. "Pertains not this" unto us neither? Is not this worth the regard? Sure if any thing be worthy the regard, this is most worthy of our very worthiest and best regard.

Thus have we considered and seen, not so much as in this sight we might or should, but as much as the time will give us leave. And now lay all these before you, every one of them a *non sicut* of itself: the pains of his body, esteemed by Pilate's *Ecce*; the sorrows of his soul, by his sweat in the garden; the comfortless estate of his sorrows, by his cry on the cross; and with these, his person, as being the Son of the Great and Eternal God. Then join to these the cause: in God, "his fierce wrath"; in us, our heinous sins deserving it; in him, his exceeding great love, both suffering that for us which we had deserved and procuring for us that we could never deserve—making that to appertain to himself which of right pertained to us, and making that pertain to us which pertained to him only, and not to us at all but by his means alone. And after their view in several,[68] lay them all together, so many *non sicut*s into one, and tell me if his complaint be not just and his request most reasonable.

Yes sure, his complaint is just: "Have ye no regard?" None? And yet never the like? None? And it pertains unto you? "No regard?" As if it were some common ordinary matter—and the like never was? "No regard?" As if it concerned you not a whit—and it toucheth you so near? As if he should say, "Rare things you regard, yea,

68. in several—separately.

though they no ways pertain to you. This is exceeding rare, and will you not regard it?" Again, things that nearly touch you, you regard, though they be not rare at all: this toucheth you exceeding near, even as near as your soul toucheth you, and will you not yet regard it? Will neither of these by itself move you? Will not both these together move you? What will move you? Will pity? Here is distress never the like. Will duty? Here is a person never the like. Will fear? Here is wrath never the like. Will remorse? Here are sins never the like. Will kindness? Here is love never the like. Will bounty? Here are benefits never the like. Will all these? Here they be all, all above any *sicut*, all in the highest degree.

Truly the complaint is just, it may move us; it wanteth no reason, it may move; and it wanteth no affection[69] in the delivery of it to us, on his part to move us. Sure it moved him exceeding much. For among all the deadly sorrows of his most bitter passion, this, even this, seemeth to be his greatest of all and that which did most affect him: even the grief of the slender reckoning most men have it in, as little respecting him, as if he had done or suffered nothing at all for them. For lo, of all the sharp pains he endureth, he complaineth not, but of this he complaineth: of no regard. That which grieveth him most, that which most he moaneth is this. It is strange he should be in pains, such pains as never any was, and not complain himself of them, but of want of regard only. Strange, he should not make request: "O deliver me!" or "Relieve me!" But only "O consider and regard me!" In effect, as if he said, "None, no deliverance, no relief do I seek; regard I seek. And all that I suffer, I am content with it; I regard it not; I suffer most willingly, if this I may find at your hands: regard."

69. affection—emotion.

Truly, this so passionate a complaint may move us; it moved all but us. For most strange of all it is that all the creatures in heaven and earth seemed to hear this his mournful complaint, and in their kind to show their regard of it. The sun in heaven shrinking in his light, the earth trembling under it, the very stones cleaving in sunder,[70] as if they had sense and sympathy of it—and sinful men only not moved with it. And yet it was not for the creatures this was done to him; to them it pertaineth not. But for us it was, and to us it doth. And shall we not yet regard it? Shall the creature, and not we? Shall we not?

If we do not, it may appertain to us, but we pertain not to it. It pertains to all, but all pertain not to it. None pertain to it but they that take benefit by it. And none take benefit by it, no more than by the brazen serpent, but they that fix their eye on it. Behold, consider, and regard it; the profit, the benefit, is lost without regard.

If we do not, as this was a day of God's "fierce wrath" against him, only for regarding us, so there is another day coming, and it will quickly be here: a day of like "fierce wrath" against us, for not regarding him. "And who regardeth the power of his wrath?" (Ps. 90:11). He that doth will surely regard this. In that day, there is not the most careless of us all but shall cry as they did in the Gospel: *Domine, non ad te pertinet, si perimus?* "Pertains it not to thee—carest thou not that we perish?" (Mark 4:38). Then would we be glad to pertain to him and his passion. Pertains it to us then, and pertains it not now? Sure now it must, if then it shall.[71]

Then to give end to this complaint, let us grant him his request and regard his passion. Let the rareness of it, the nearness to us, let pity or duty, fear or remorse, love or bounty—any of

70. Cf. Matt. 27:51; Luke 23:45.

71. Although he maintains a practical focus on the present, Andrewes often makes the final judgment the ultimate horizon for his preaching: "Our charge is to preach to men, *non quae volunt audire, sed quae volunt audisse,* not what for the present

them or all of them—let the justness of his complaint, let his affectionate manner of complaining of this and only this, let the shame of the creatures' regard, let our profit or our peril, let something prevail with us to have it in some regard. Some regard! Verily, as his sufferings, his love, our good by them are, so should our regard be a *non sicut* too—that is, a regard of these, and of nothing in comparison of these. It should be so, for with the benefit ever the regard should arise.

But God help us poor sinners, and be merciful unto us! Our regard is a *non sicut* indeed, but it is backward, and in a contrary sense, that is, no where so shallow, so short, or so soon done. It should be otherwise, it should have our deepest consideration this, and our highest regard. But if that cannot be had, our nature is so heavy, and flesh and blood so dull of apprehension in spiritual things, yet at leastwise some regard. Some, I say—the more the better, but in any wise some, and not as here no regard, none at all. Some ways to show we make account of it: to withdraw ourselves, to void our minds of other matters, to set this before us, to think upon it, to thank him for it, to regard him—and stay and see whether he will regard us or no. Sure he will, and we shall feel our "hearts pricked" with sorrow (Acts 2:37), by consideration of the cause in us—our sin—and again "warm within us" (Luke 24:32), by consideration of the cause in him—his love—till by some motion of grace he answer us, and show that our regard is accepted of him.

And this, as at all other times (for no day is amiss but at all times some time to be taken for this duty), so specially on this day—this day, which we hold holy to the memory of his passion—this day to do it: to make this day, the day of God's wrath and Christ's suffering, a day

they would hear, but what another day they would wish they had heard" (Ash Wednesday 1619, 1:358).

to us of serious consideration and regard of them both.

It is kindly to consider *opus diei in die suo,* "the work of the day in the day it was wrought"; and this day it was wrought. This day therefore, whatsoever business be, to lay them aside a little; whatsoever our haste, yet to stay a little, and to spend a few thoughts in calling to mind and taking to regard what this day the Son of God did and suffered for us; and all for this end, that what he was then we might not be, and what he is now we might be forever. Which Almighty God grant we may do, more or less, even every one of us, according to the several measures of his grace in us!

CHAPTER 5

Selected Sermons

Maybe the most important thing to say about the sermons that follow is that in each of them I assume that my congregation is interested in the text they have just heard. Since that is my regular working assumption, I always preach exegetically. This is worth mentioning, because exegetical preaching is rare in our time—and often, I am told, preachers are advised against it. Yet I consistently find, when teaching and preaching in various settings, that people are really interested in what the text says, even if they don't have much prior knowledge of the Bible.

So the second thing I would say is that I do not preach in a fundamentally different way to an "average congregation" than I do when addressing my own students (although they are the congregation I most frequently address). When I am speaking to theology students, I can of course make certain references (e.g., to "the Elohist") without explanation, but this is a superficial difference. After all, every preacher who speaks regularly to a congregation uses a certain amount of "insider" language. The crucial point is that the text is in fact inherently interesting, and because I stick close to it, I do not have the common worry of "finding a story" to *add* interest to the sermon. (It seems to me that such an approach resembles the food industry's practice of adding nutritive "enhancers" to foods from which the nutritional value has been stripped in processing.) The passage itself provides the story. Even if it is not a narrative, it is always a point of entry into the larger biblical story, and that is where I direct the attention of my hearers.

These sermons are not offered as models; they are representative samples of ways I have worked with both poetic and narrative texts. Because

I am most often preaching in settings where a lectionary is used (either the Episcopal Church Lectionary or the Revised Common Lectionary), the central text is generally chosen for me. Although I usually focus on only one of the texts appointed for a given day, I sometimes make reference to other passages (appointed or not) that illumine my main preaching text. The sermons appear here without change of reference to the particular circumstances in which they were preached.

Genesis 21:1–21

Marquand Chapel, Yale Divinity School
January 30, 1996

Episcopal Church Lectionary, Tuesday of IV Epiphany, Year II

One senses that the narrator we nickname "the Elohist" would prefer not to have to tell this story of Abraham and his rivalrous women. None of the traditional heroes comes off looking very good. Not Sarah, with whom we would like to sympathize—both because she is our adoptive mother and because she bore for decades the curse and shame of infertility. But our sympathy cannot countenance her cruelty: she evidently watches with some satisfaction as a young woman walks off into the arid wilderness of Be'er Sheva, carrying a waterskin, a loaf of bread, and a child—the child who is an intolerable competitor to the newborn crown prince, Isaac.

Nor does Abraham look much better for caving in to Sarah's tyrannical jealousy. Nor does God look very good, for telling Abraham it's okay. This is not one of God's more salvific moments: "Listen to [Sarah], for it is through Isaac that seed will be named for you. Besides, I'll take care of the slave woman's son; I'll make him a nation, too, since he is your seed" (vv. 12–13). It sounds less like promise than afterthought, this arrangement God makes for "the slave woman's son."

This narrative is sometimes regarded as the acme of triumphalist apologetics. It is said to be a story told "from the oppressor's perspective";[1] the Elohist rejects Hagar and the son he does not even deign to name in favor of the party line: "It is through Isaac that seed will be named for [Abraham]." But I am not convinced that the Elohist lacks interest in Hagar. If so, then why should he make her plight so memorable? For

---

1. Phyllis Trible, *Texts of Terror*, OBT 13 (Philadelphia: Fortress, 1984), 9.

Sarah and Abraham, perhaps, it is "out of sight, out of mind"—though I doubt it. The people we have treated the worst generally have a disturbing persistence in our memories. But certainly we readers and hearers of the biblical narrative are not allowed to forget how Hagar has been treated and how God now treats her in the wilderness.

We cannot forget, because we are there. We watch Hagar toss the child's body under a bush (וַתַּשְׁלֵךְ [*vattashlekh*]); the verb is used elsewhere of discarding a corpse (שׁלך [*sh-l-kh*]; see, e.g., Josh. 8:29). We see precisely where she sits—about a bowshot away, far enough not to hear the boy's weakening cries. We hear the only words Hagar ever speaks: "Let me not watch the child die" (v. 16). It's part prayer and mostly abandonment to despair, for with those words Hagar in effect forfeits her motherhood. She does not name Ishmael or even name him as hers; he's just "the child"—who is dying. הַיֶּלֶד (*hayyeled*), "the child"—that detached phrase captures the ultimate horror of Hagar's situation: the slave woman is reduced to giving up what she must see as her only claim to human dignity, her status as mother and protector of Ishmael. Once she has forfeited that, her own death cannot be far away.

And then the angel speaks: מַה־לָּךְ הָגָר (*mah-lakh hagar*), "What's with you, Hagar?" The angel recalls her first to herself—"What's going on with you, Hagar?"—and then recalls her to motherhood: "'Rise, pick up the child and hold him tight, for I shall make him into a great nation.' And God opened her eyes and she saw a water well; and she went and filled the waterskin and gave the child to drink" (vv. 17–19). The sparse wilderness of Paran proves to be a place of life and independence for Hagar and the boy Ishmael. God is with him there, he grows to be a bowman, his mother takes for him an Egyptian wife (vv. 20–21). It is the beginning of the tribe of Ishmael, also known as *bedouin*, the tribe of Arabic-speaking desert dwellers.

Hagar is an unforgettable image of victimhood, as is evidenced by the number of painters who have chosen her as a subject. They have chosen her, I imagine, to represent the victimization of women and men of every culture and age, people debased by cruelty and hopelessness below what they could recognize as their own humanity; people restored to hope, to responsibility, to life by God's utterly surprising action. As a subject of religious art, Hagar is a universal symbol of victimhood and restoration, and it is a fair use of her story.

But within the context of Israel's story—in Scripture—she stands for more than that, for something much more specific than that. The clue to what she stands for is given in the repeated note that Hagar is an Egyptian slave (16:1, 3; 21:9–10). I believe the narrative means to show Hagar as a kind of dark mirror held up to Israel's face. Hagar the Egyptian slave is the reverse image of Israel, itself to be enslaved in Egypt. You might call her the "shadow side" of the chosen people, and the particular words and themes chosen for Hagar's story develop that correspondence. Sarah *afflicts* her pregnant maid (וַתְּעַנֶּהָ [*vatte anneha*], 16:6), exactly as Pharaoh's taskmasters will one day afflict the Israelites, who are likewise all too successful at having babies (Exod. 1:11–12).[2] Eventually the mere sight of Ishmael playing pushes Sarah over the edge, and she gives the order: "*Drive out* this slave and her son." גֵּרֵשׁ (*garash*), "drive out"—it is the same word used of the Israelite slaves, driven out of Egypt after the tenth plague, the death of the firstborn (Exod. 12:29). There's a grim correspondence and contrast also in this matter of the *firstborn*.

Sarah drives out the slave after the birth of her own first son; Pharaoh, after the death of all Egypt's firstborn. Sarah evidently doesn't trust God to protect the chosen one. Ironically, Pharaoh acts precisely because he now knows that God will stop at nothing in looking out for God's own. In both cases, of course, the slaves are expelled into the *wilderness*, where Hagar's experience is a foreshadowing of Israel's: the wandering, the deadly thirst, the miraculous provision of water where there seemed to be none before.

I realize this is more concordance work than you are accustomed to even in an Area One[3] sermon, but it's only when you catch all the echoes that you get the point, namely, this: Hagar the Egyptian slave looks eerily like Israel in Egypt, that is, paradigmatic Israel, Israel when it has the strongest claim on God's saving action, Israel when it is afflicted, endangered, desperate. Hagar looks like Israel oppressed, and Sarah, the mother of all Israel, is her oppressor. This is stunning. With this story Israel goes on record that from the beginning it has an identity as oppressor as well as oppressed. In Sarah, Israel learned something of what it means to be oppressor, even before Israel went down into Egypt to suffer oppression there.

I want to stress that this is not a counterreading of the text, nor is it a subtle reading. All these points are quite obvious if you are working with the Hebrew text and know a little about the conventions of biblical narrative. It is just because this reading is not very high-tech that I

---

2. Also note that Sarai means "princess"; in Exodus, the Egyptians appoint שָׂרִים (*sarim*), "taskmasters," over Israel (1:11).

3. The area of the curriculum to which biblical courses and faculty are assigned.

cannot agree that Hagar's narrator is a party-line election theologian who regards her as a throwaway character in salvation history. On the contrary, in Hagar, the mother of the Arab nations, Israel finds a compelling and disturbing image of itself.

The amazing thing is that Israel memorializes that correspondence in its Scriptures; you might say that Israel holds its fiercest rival ever in its own face (cf. 16:12). A story like this one is strong grounds on which to argue the divine inspiration of Scripture, for it is impossible to believe that any people would tell this story about themselves and their enemies because they liked to tell it. The story of Hagar is about the downside of election theology; it puts forth in poignant terms the case of Israel's enemies against Israel. With this narrative, Israel forces itself to confront Hagar's claim on God's saving action. It puts that claim before the world and even before God (for Jewish tradition teaches that God studies Torah up in heaven just as we study it here). This story of Hagar is evidence that part of the cost of worshiping Israel's God is living with your rivals in your face, being forced to reckon with the very real claims of the great nation that comes from Hagar and her son Ishmael—that is, the numberless nation of the less favored, the people who do not stand under a clear sign of promise but must settle for experiencing God's blessing at the margins of history.

Something happens when we, who commonly identify ourselves with Israel, keep the Ishmaelites' story before us as we press our own claims upon God. Something becomes evident to which we would otherwise be blind, namely, how much forbearance we daily experience from that great nation of the less favored—sometimes known as our enemies. That we do not generally perceive our less-favored brothers and sisters as our enemies, that we live with them in relative peace—that is due far more to their forbearance than to our efforts at peacemaking.

It is due to the forbearance of the Ishmaelites that our ghettoes are not perpetually in flames. For many of us, it is due to forbearance that our families are not in constant turmoil—for everyone in a family is not equally favored, by either nature or nurture. Also here at YDS we live by forbearance. We count on the people who clean our halls, our bathrooms, our classrooms, and our offices not to resent us—indeed, we count on them to like us who, in many cases by accident of birth, have opportunities they lack. In the sphere of world history, we are now witnessing acts of forbearance that begin to heal the ancient rivalry between Hagar and Sarah, the mothers of the Palestinians and the Jews. Palestinians and Israelis shaking hands, doing business, honoring Yitzhak

Rabin—that's forbearance on both sides. A Palestinian mother handing two-year-old Yusef to an Israeli soldier for a final photo opportunity during the withdrawal from Bethlehem last month—that is forbearance, and it shows that the lesson of our biblical story has not been completely missed. There is an alternative to driving out the slave woman and her son; the two peoples sprung from Abraham's loins can find a way to live together.

But sometimes one of the less favored does not forbear and strikes out in violent rage. A New York City store is set to the torch or sprayed with gunfire; an Israeli bus is bombed. Much more often, some anonymous Ishmael beats his wife, abuses her child. We for our part are quick to condemn such acts of violence, which we term "arbitrary." We are right to condemn them, for they threaten to undo all possibility of common life. But we are wrong to call them "arbitrary." That label is nothing more than a sop to our complacency, expressing our judgment that nothing fundamental must change. Thus we put the whole burden on the Ishmaelites to go back to forbearance, so we may go back to enjoying our privileged peace.

Complacency is our most common response to forbearance, and it is a particularly vicious form of ingratitude. Complacency takes the gift of peace as our due, failing to acknowledge that it is a gift, and that the gift is given for a purpose. It's meant to motivate some change in us. The proper response to the forbearance of others is repentance, *metanoia*, a total change of mind. Forbearance—and likewise occasional breaches of forbearance—should prompt us to a radical reexamination of our situation in light of what we can now understand of the situation of the Ishmaelites, the great nation of the less favored. The connection between the forbearance we receive and the repentance we undertake—that connection is crucial; quite possibly it's the master key to life in community—and of course I did not figure out that connection myself. You will recall that Paul instructs the Roman Christians: "Do you despise the riches of [God's] kindness and forbearance and patience? Do you not realize that . . . kindness is meant to lead you to repentance?" (Rom. 2:4 NRSV; cf. 2 Pet. 3:9). Though Paul is speaking specifically of God's forbearance, I think the issue is no different when our fellow human beings are the agents of the divine mercy of forbearance. Do you not know that the riches of kindness and forbearance and patience are meant to lead you to repentance?

Repentance is the steady work of those who worship Israel's God, both Christians and Jews. Hagar's story is given us as a stimulus to repentance, and she even offers us the beginnings of a prayer that can orient us to that work and, God willing, speed our change of mind. Hagar gives God a new name; she is in fact the only person in Scripture who does so. A few chapters back in Genesis, she named God אֵל רֳאִי (ʾel roʾî), "God of my seeing" (16:13). "God of my seeing"—in the landscape of death, God enabled Hagar to see the well that meant life for herself and her son, and through him life for the great nation of the less favored. Pray that the God Hagar knew may grant us the sight that enables life, life in abundance, for all Abraham's children. To the children of Ishmael, God grant courage and the solid hope that is the fruit of endurance by faith (Rom. 5:4). To those marked for privilege, grant true repentance, amendment of life, and the generosity that is the fruit of gratitude. Amen.

THE TEXT IN PREACHING CONTEXT

The story of how God, Abraham, and Sarah "deal with" Hagar presents obvious ethical difficulty, and here I proceed from the assumption that the biblical narrator *expects* us to be troubled by what we read. Our instinctive response in such a situation is often to set the text aside and preach on something that has more obvious potential to edify the church. Here I take the opposite approach: close reading of the narrative, first showing the care with which the narrator enables us to observe Hagar's plight at close range, and then showing how multiple echoes with the Exodus account shape our theological understanding of this story. Contrary to one common interpretation, the story of Hagar the Egyptian does not offer a simple endorsement of a doctrine of Israel's election—but neither does it dismiss that doctrine, which, for all its problems, is too central to the biblical understanding of reality to be discarded. Rather, by directing the reader mindful of the tradition to the Exodus story, this account of the Egyptian woman's painful expulsion subtly presses us to expand our moral vision.

In every sermon, I am looking for a reading of my text that is compatible with the gospel. Here the key I find is Paul's notion that forbearance is constitutive of Christian community. Forbearance is the quality of love (Eph. 4:2; Col. 3:13–14) that enables us deeply flawed human beings to live together in (relative) peace. Christian forbearance is a mode of living in the presence of the God who both requires our perpetual transformation and makes transformation possible.

The following "collect" (prayer) guided my preparation. It was read immediately after the sermon, as a way of gathering the congregation's attention and directing it to the kind of transformation that God requires of us:

> O God, you made us in your own image and redeemed us through Jesus your Son: Look with compassion on the whole human family; take away the arrogance and hatred which infect our hearts; break down the walls that separate us; unite us in bonds of love; and work through our struggle and confusion to accomplish your purposes on earth; that, in your good time, all nations and races may serve you in harmony around your heavenly throne; through Jesus Christ our Lord. *Amen.*[4]

---

4. Collect for the Human Family, *BCP*, 815.

Isaiah 5:8–25

Virginia Theological Seminary Chapel
December 7, 1998

Episcopal Church Lectionary, Monday of II Advent, Year I

Verses in roman type are appointed for Monday of II Advent; verses in italics are appointed for Tuesday of II Advent.

Isa. 5:8 Woe to those who join house to house, link field to field,
until there is no room,
and you are settled by yourselves in the middle of
the land!
9 In my ears [swears] the LORD of Hosts,
"Surely many houses will become a devastation,
big ones, good ones, be without inhabitant.
10 For ten acres of vineyard will yield a single *bat*
and a *homer* of seed will yield but an *ephah*."
11 Woe to those who rise early in the morning and chase after
strong drink;
still late in the evening, wine enflames them.
12 And they have lyre and harp, drum and pipe,
and the wine of their drinking bouts;
but the action of the LORD they do not consider,
and the work of his hands they do not see.
13 *Therefore my people goes into exile for want of*
knowledge;
its honored men are dying of hunger,
its common folk parched with thirst.
14 *Therefore Sheol has widened its gullet*
and opened its mouth without limit.

138

> And down go Jerusalem's splendor and her crowd,
>   the roar and the exultation in her.
> ¹⁵ People bowed down, humanity brought low,
>   and eyes of lofty ones cast down.
> ¹⁶ But lofty is the LORD of Hosts in justice, in judgment [מִשְׁפָּט
>   (mishpat)],
>   and the Holy God is hallowed in righteousness.
> ¹⁷ Lambs shall graze as in their pasture,
>   and in the ruins fatlings and kids feed.
> ¹⁸ Woe to those who draw iniquity with cords of evil
>   and sin like a cart rope.
> ¹⁹ Who say, "Let it hurry,
>   let his work be quick, so that we may see it!
>   Let it approach, let it come,
>   the purpose of the Holy One of Israel, that we may know it!"
> ²⁰ Woe to those who call evil good and good evil,
>   who put darkness for light and light for darkness,
>   who put bitter for sweet and sweet for bitter.
> ²¹ Woe to those who are wise in their own eyes,
>   and shrewd in their own sight!
> ²² Woe to the heroes in drinking wine,
>   men valorous in mixing strong drink.
> ²³ Who justify the guilty for a bribe
>   but deprive the righteous of their right.
> ²⁴ Therefore as a tongue of fire devours stubble,
>   and as dry grass sinks in the flame,
>   so their root will be as rottenness,
>   their blossom go up like dust,
>   for they have despised the teaching of the LORD of Hosts,
>   the word of the Holy One of Israel they have reviled.
> ²⁵ Therefore the wrath of the LORD burned against his people,
>   and he stretched out his hand against them and struck.
>   And the mountains shook and their corpses
>   are like dung in the middle of the streets.
>   For all this his anger is not turned back,
>   and his hand is stretched out still.

Some scholars opine that Jesus was born, not in winter, but in spring— unquestionably, a more probable time for shepherds to be camped out near Bethlehem. Yet the church calendar has located this season of Advent accurately, in spiritual if not in historical terms. For Advent is a deep winter season, a dark time of the Christian year—dark with mystery, but dark also, as the readings and prayers for today force us to see, because this is a season of sober reckoning with our sin. It is fitting that Advent comes at what is normally the coldest time of year, in Israel as in Virginia. "Ice condenses on the bone"[5] when Isaiah blasts us with the reality of human sin:

> Woe to those who call evil good and good evil,
> who put darkness for light and light for darkness,
> who put bitter for sweet and sweet for bitter.
> Woe to those who are wise in their own eyes,
> and shrewd in their own sight!
>
> *(vv. 20–21)*

> . . . my people goes into exile for want of knowledge;
> its honored men are dying of hunger,
> its common folk parched with thirst.
> . . . Sheol has widened its gullet.
> . . . .
> And down go Jerusalem's splendor and her crowd.
> . . . .
> People bowed down, humanity brought low.
> . . . .
> But lofty is the LORD of Hosts in *justice*, in *judgment*,
> and the Holy God is hallowed in righteousness.
>
> *(vv. 13–16)*

"Thanks be to God." Our liturgical response implies that we should be grateful for the gift of this "word of the LORD," but why? Searching for our own gratitude draws us into the great paradox of Advent, and it is this: the winter solstice of human sin calls forth the Light of the World. God answers our deepest darkness with the blaze of heaven's light. It happened once in ancient Palestine, but the Advent paradox is not really a historical phenomenon. No, it is an enduring and demanding reality in which we must learn to live. The searing readings and the bold prayers of this season attest that the blaze of heaven has not yet died down, though we be oblivious to it. At an unexpected hour, that burn-

---

5. W. H. Auden, "For the Time Being: A Christmas Oratorio" (1941–1942), in *Collected Poems*, ed. Edward Mendelson (New York: Random House, 1976), 271.

ing light will again burst upon us when our Lord comes in judgment, and wickedness will be consumed in the blaze:

> As a tongue of fire devours stubble,
> and as dry grass sinks in the flame,
> so their root will be as rottenness,
> their blossom go up like dust,
> for they have despised the teaching of the Lord of Hosts,
> the word of the Holy One of Israel they have reviled.
>
> *(v. 24)*

Now, much of what I have just repeated from the Isaiah reading you were in fact not intended to hear today, according to the lectionary. Oddly, the lectionary does some complicated dissection and division of this passage. (I've taken the very un-Anglican step of giving you a Bible handout in church, so you can see what has been cut.) If we had read only what was appointed for today, we would have heard only Isaiah's pronouncements of woe. Then separately, tomorrow, we would have read what Isaiah intertwines with those woes—namely, the picture of our Holy God exalted, exalted in מִשְׁפָּט (*mishpat*), which means both judgment and justice. The reasoning behind this dissection of Isaiah's oracle is, I confess, too subtle for me. But its effect I think I understand. The condemnation of sin—the woes—is completely cut off from the one thing that enables us to look at sin squarely, as Isaiah would have us do, to look at sin without falling into total despair. And that is the assertion that over and above our sin God is exalted in מִשְׁפָּט (*mishpat*), in judgment and in justice. It is imperative that we contemplate both these things at the same time—our sin and our exalted God—if we are to embrace the real hope that this season holds. The central theological image of the season, the image of God in Christ coming "in his glorious majesty to judge both the quick and the dead"[6]—that is meant to be a hopeful image. But the hope it expresses is a real and not facile element of the church's faith only if we are willing to reckon squarely and indeed painfully with our sin.

As theologians, we must feel the acute pressure either to demonstrate the good news in the picture of Christ coming in judgment or to drop that article of the Creed. For, unlike the baby Jesus, the image of Christ exalted as judge of the world has proven to have no commercial value whatsoever and therefore no grip on the popular imagination—including, I think it is fair to say, the popular religious imagination in

6. Collect for the First Sunday of Advent, *BCP*, 159.

mainstream Protestant churches. So why should we continue daily to affirm that Jesus Christ is coming to judge the world? Where is the hope in that? Here: Christ coming in judgment means that the power of evil is finite. Powerful though the grip of evil is upon us all, squeezing us from within and without, deforming the image of God in us, blinding us to that image in our neighbor—though evil's grip is death dealing, it is also temporary, penultimate. By definition, there is only one ultimate thing, and that is God's grip upon the world and all that is in it. Isaiah sees God exalted in מִשְׁפָּט (mishpat), in judgment and in justice. Thus Isaiah, hardly a facile optimist, assures us that God's purpose for creation—justice—will finally prevail. All contrary purposes, all devices that distort God's design and maim God's creatures, will vanish in the judgment of God—like burnt stubble, like rottenness, like dust. All false purposes will be exposed for the utter unreality they are, when at the last every creature stands in the immediate presence of the Holy One of Israel. For is that not what the final judgment/the final justice is: every creature standing in the immediate presence of the Holy One of Israel?

Thus God exalted in judgment is indeed a hopeful image of the finiteness of evil—but *for whom* is it hopeful? On this point Isaiah leaves us in no doubt at all. The judgment and justice of God is good news for the poor and powerless, who have been deprived of their right under the grip of evil. God exalted in judgment—that is woe for the movers and shakers, the opinion makers who get away with "call[ing] evil good and good evil" (v. 20). God's judgment is woe for the wealthy—and in Isaiah's terms, that would include most of us. Woe to us who call evil good. We call "healthy" a rapacious global economy that may succeed in growing our pension fund investments, yet at the same time the hope of the poor in this nation and countless others ebbs steadily—hope of having decent homes and schools, unpolluted water and soil; hope that their children's lives will not be cut short by violence, distorted by drugs, frustrated by joblessness. Woe to us who call good evil, as the advertising industry has taught us to do, convincing us that taking no more than we need of the world's goods is not the good practice of temperance but rather the evil of deprivation. Woe to us who call darkness light, who have learned to call our habitual overconsumption "comfort," or even "joy," rather than what the Bible terms it: avarice, which is the root of all evil (1 Tim. 6:10), because avarice can finally be satisfied only through various forms of violence and oppression—often officially sanctioned, fully legal violence.

Isaiah's "woes" confront us, who are not poor and powerless, with the uncertainty of our situation before the Holy One of Israel. Who knows whether we will stand or fall at the last? But this we do know: we have now an opportunity—heeding the warning of the prophets, we have an opportunity to move closer to the poor and powerless, to claim their interest, their cause, more fully as our own. We have in fact been prepared for this opportunity by our daily prayer throughout the year:

> Let not the needy, O Lord, be forgotten;
> Nor the hope of the poor be taken away.[7]

If we are serious about not depriving the poor of hope, then we must believe that the judgment of God is good news, and find ways to proclaim it. Moreover, if the hope of the poor is not to be taken away in our time—taken away by us—then we must let our own lives be conditioned by that ultimate reality. Submitting ourselves while in this world to the final judgment of God is possibly the most difficult work of a disciplined theological imagination, and the most important. Therefore, we must seek reliable guidance, holy images to deepen our imagining, to deepen our prayer for the total defeat of evil, including the evil within ourselves.

When I say "holy images," I'm talking, in part at least, about pictures. The judgment of God used to be one of the most common themes for artists, but now almost no one takes up the challenge of helping the modern religious imagination encounter that reality. Yet I can think of one such image: in Coventry Cathedral, Graham Sutherland's great tapestry weaving of Christ enthroned as judge and ruler of the universe. Seventy-five feet high, it dominates the whole nave. I don't think anyone would call that imposing work of art "pretty." The strong green background is too assertive; the steel-grey lines of the design are sharply drawn, symmetrical. The image compels rather than invites attention. The huge seated Christ looks too much like a Palestinian man who has recently been crucified; the wounds on his upraised hands and bare feet are still raw. Yet that tapestry hangs behind the altar as a tremendous, unavoidable pronouncement of good news. This news: that the reign of evil is finite and coming to an end in this world. In Coventry, that statement has immediate historical interest. For outside the present nave stands the ruin of the fifteenth-century Church of St. Michael, destroyed by Blitz bombers in 1940. One enters the cathedral building through the ruin. Standing before the altar of fallen stones, no one can overlook the problem of human evil. In the heart of a medieval city that was nearly leveled in one November night, this bombed-out but still functional

---

7. *BCP*, 55.

sanctuary testifies to the reality that through baptism, Christians actively enlist in God's battle against "Satan and all the spiritual forces of wickedness."[8] Then, turning 90 degrees from the altar in the ruin, one looks through a great glass wall etched with the bodies of saints and angels, into the newly built nave. At its far end rises the immense figure of Christ in glory.

The evangelical design of Coventry Cathedral speaks with particular power in this season of Advent. For this is the architecture of Advent. See, the two poles of the design are the bombed ruin and the enthroned Christ. Standing at the edge of the ruin, we can just glimpse the figure of Christ, sober, wounded by sin, exalted as judge and ruler of the world. That image becomes more clear as one passes among the translucent bodies of saints and angels that separate the ruin from the new nave. The whole design rests upon those two structuring elements of Advent— the ruin worked by sin and the exalted Christ—the structuring elements with which we begin again now, as we do each year, to define the Christian experience.

Advent forces us to be realistic about our situation, our ministry; it locates us in the ruin of human sin. As long as we are in this world, we will never go more than a few steps outside that ruin. Some Christians are called to minister in the places of greatest damage their whole life long, painstakingly building altars with fallen stones. Inevitably, we discover that some serious damage has been worked within us; then, the process of clearing rubble and rebuilding is personally painful. The work is slow, unremitting, the results uncertain, and the light not good. Yet (and this is crucial) none of us works wholly in the dark. For once the full blaze of heaven's glory shot through the darkness, and it has not been extinguished. By that light we can see enough to work well even in the midst of ruin. And more—lifting our eyes, we can see beyond it. Gazing through the translucent bodies of saints and angels, we glimpse the figure of Christ, sober, wounded by sin, exalted in justice, in judgment. May that vision so condition our life now that we may at the last greet with joy the day of his coming. Amen.

THE TEXT IN PREACHING CONTEXT

This sermon is wholly conditioned by the season in which it was preached. Throughout Advent, the (Episcopal Church) lectionary empha-

---

8. *BCP*, 302.

sizes readings from the Prophets. This year (Year I of the Daily Office cycle), we read each day from Isaiah. The tone of the lessons for the first ten days (this sermon was preached on the ninth day of Advent) consistently challenges the church's complacency. A hymn sung at the service captures the essence of the challenge:

> What is the crying at Jordan?
> Who hears, O God, the prophecy?
> Dark is the season, dark our hearts
> and shut to mystery.
>
> Who then shall stir in this darkness,
> prepare for joy in the winter night?
> Mortal in darkness we lie down,
> blind-hearted seeing no light.[9]

The notion that the sternness of the prophetic message is meant to "prepare [us] for joy" is expressed also in the collect prayed during the second week of Advent:

> Merciful God, who sent your messengers the prophets to preach repentance and prepare the way for our salvation: Give us grace to heed their warnings and forsake our sins, that we may greet with joy the coming of Jesus Christ our Redeemer; who lives and reigns with you and the Holy Spirit, one God, now and for ever. Amen.[10]

Both my translation of Isaiah and the sermon itself highlight the fact that the Hebrew word מִשְׁפָּט (*mishpat*) means both "judgment" and "justice." Those two aspects of God's action and character are generally separated in our modern theological understanding, with a distinct preference for the latter. Their separation seems to be endorsed by the lectionary's unusual—and in my view, erratic—division of the text, which means that the "woes," the oracles of judgment (Isa. 5:8–12, 18–23) are no longer heard in conjunction with the picture of God exalted as Just Judge (v. 16). The sermon aims at restoring the integrity of the text, thereby making intelligible its communication of good news.

---

9. "What Is the Crying at Jordan," words by Carol Christopher Drake. *The Hymnal 1982* of the Episcopal Church, USA (New York: Church Hymnal Corp., 1985), no. 69.
10. Collect for the Second Sunday of Advent, BCP, 211.

Psalm 1

York Chapel, Duke Divinity School
February 18, 2004

Revised Common Lectionary, VI Epiphany, Year C

Happy is the one who has not walked
in the counsel of the wicked,
and in the way of sinners has not stood,
and in the sitting-place of the scornful has not sat;
but in the Torah of YHWH is his delight,
and on [God's] Teaching she meditates day and night.

Ps. 1:1–2

Strange that the Psalter, the prayer book of Israel, should begin this way, with a psalm that is not a prayer at all but rather a wisdom poem, a statement about the spiritual life composed probably by some ancient academic. The contrast with what follows is striking. Most of the psalms are anything but ivory-tower pronouncements. They are impassioned cries of anguish and victory from people fighting in the trenches—both literal and metaphorical trenches. Yet the preface to those prayers comes from a place something like this one, a place where "happy" people study Torah, delightedly toiling night and day over the Teaching of God.

Okay, I admit it: "happy" is not the best translation for the first word of this psalm, אַשְׁרֵי (ʾashrê). "Fortunate" is more like it; even better, "privileged." Here the psalmist is making a more or less objective statement about quality of life. Studying God's Teaching is what constitutes the good life, though it is not invariably a feel-good activity. אַשְׁרֵי (ʾashrê), "*Privileged* is the one who meditates on Torah day and night"—this is not a democratic picture of the good life, like the prophetic ideal of every Israelite sitting under his own vine and fig tree (Mic. 4:4; Zech.

3:10; 1 Kings 5:5 [4:25 Eng.]; etc.). No, it's a picture of privilege; here, standing apart from the presumably large group gathered in "the sitting-place of the scornful," are the privileged few who find pure delight in studying the Torah of YHWH.

Well, okay, maybe it is not always *pure* delight. You could translate that fifth line less rapturously: "And with the Torah of YHWH is his *business.*" The privileged life belongs to the relatively few who make it their business to pore over Scripture day and night, whether they are in the mood for it or not. So here we are, beloved of the Lord, all of us victims of the good life.

That is, of course, exactly what you would expect a professorial preacher to say. Yet the psalms were not written by academics looking for one more way to give their students a hard time. They were written by and for people who pray, for people who want more than anything else to know God, at least a little; for people who want to spend time with God, at least a little time every day, so that (as one lovely prayer for the morning says) "in all the cares and occupations of our life we may not forget you [God], but may remember that we are ever walking in your sight."[11] And since the Psalter is a book for people who pray, this first psalm, like any good preface, tells us what we need to know from the outset in order to make sense of the rest of the book. Now happily for us, the author of the first psalm took a sort of *Psalter for Dummies* approach to the task. The psalm makes only one point, and makes it really clear: you're not going to get anywhere in the life of prayer unless you're reading Scripture, God's Torah, all the time.

Perhaps it is coincidence, but the fact that the psalms appear in the middle of the Bible suggests to me what is in fact the case: that genuine prayer emerges out of the midst of the Scriptures, out of reading and rereading them. Our prayers deepen—they may substantively change—as we become better readers of the Word. From a biblical perspective, that is the process of prayer. And if that is not our process, then we may pray and pray, but if we are not growing through ever deeper study of God's Torah, growing strong roots like a tree planted by water channels, then our prayers simply will not be fruitful.

So we pray standing in the middle of the Bible, with the stories and images of Scripture flowing around us like streams of water, helping us grow as we pray. The ancient poets who composed the psalms knew that, of course, and as we pray their words, we find that people we

---

11. A Collect for Guidance, BCP, 100.

know through Scripture attend us as we pray, and their stories shape our prayers. I may pray alongside David, crying out to God in bitter anguish, because someone who used to love me now hates me and seeks to destroy me. Or I pray with David in the anguish (no less bitter) of really seeing my own sin. Sometimes I pray with Hannah, whom rabbinic tradition rightly honors as one of the great prayer warriors of the Bible, as I first plead with God to hear my heart's desire and then glorify the God who bends down and listens to the prayer of the heartbroken (cf. Pss. 113, 130). Jeremiah also prays with me—that most beleaguered of the prophets, whose cries to God so often sound like psalms of lament. And always, I pray the psalms with and through Jesus Christ, whose own words to God are transparent to his regular practice of praying the psalms. Jesus prays them in the presence of strong enemies. (And what doesn't the psalmist know about praying in the presence of enemies?) Jesus prays them when he feels abandoned by God. (The psalmist knows that territory too.) Thus praying the psalms in the company of Jesus and all these saints, we learn to pray boldly, yet without sentimentality or self-deception.

But praying like that doesn't come naturally; it takes a lot of practice, daily practice over a long period of time. Therefore, it involves a choice, which the first psalm presents in stark terms. Either we form daily habits that enable us to grow slowly in God and the things of God, or we yield, by tiny increments, to the insubstantial life that is, after all, the norm. In the psalmist's society and in ours, countless lives are governed by whim, by fascination with and anxiety over things that are passing away. The final judgment of the psalm is uncompromising: life that is not rooted in the things of God, "the way of the wicked," as the psalmist bluntly calls it—that way vanishes without a trace. The statement is bald, but as so often in the psalms, it confirms a truth we have seen from our own experience. We've all known and probably loved people whose admirable qualities and even noble aspirations finally yielded nothing of lasting value. The desire to be good and do good, unless made firm by holy discipline, is with tragic frequency obliterated in personal chaos.

The church as a whole is about to enter the great season of holy discipline, Lent, and so this is a good time to take up the psalmist's challenge to make a difficult decision about the company we keep. Yet at first glance it seems that none of us is personally challenged by the warning against sitting "in the sitting-place of the scornful." Even if we wanted to keep racy company these days, those folks wouldn't want to hang out with us, so perforce we all keep company with moderately godly people—each other. But Christians have long recognized that if the literal interpretation of a psalm doesn't touch us closely, then we should try a less literal one. So I propose that in our culture, in Christian homes and even in our homes, the functional equivalent of "the sitting-place of the scornful" is often the easy chair in front of the television set.

After all, who are these "scornful," who present such a threat? Whoever would distract us from giving our best attention to God; whoever would hurt us by filling our thoughts and imagination with things that have no substance, so that we become in the end "like chaff, which the wind drives about" (v. 4). And most of what is on television—doesn't it do exactly that? It invades our imagination, the human faculty that has the greatest potential for connecting us with God. It fills our minds with what our ancestors called "vain imaginings," powerful yet empty fantasies unconnected to God and the real aching world that even now Jesus Christ is working to reconcile with God (cf. Rom. 5:10; 2 Cor. 5:19; Col. 1:20). Last week Peter Storey told me of the change that American television has wrought in the new generation of black South Africans: "What the kids want now is the Nikes they see on TV. Their parents are wringing their hands. They risked their lives, and now their children are mall-crazy."

Television as a global case of "bad company" may seem a long way from your own life of prayer, but let me suggest that precisely because you pray, this is a good place to exercise countercultural vigilance—even, to use a traditional word, to practice asceticism. I'm not saying you should never sit in front of the television (although that might be a good idea for the six weeks of Lent). But when you do sit there, get in the habit of asking a question that almost no one around the globe asks: What is it costing me to sit here? The two most likely answers are ones that should give prayerful people pause. It is costing you time you might otherwise spend in sleep, thus depriving you of one of the sweetest gifts of God. As the psalmist says elsewhere, God "gives to his beloved sleep" (Ps. 127:2). A second answer: it is costing you time you might spend in stillness, sitting quietly with the Word of God in your hand or your heart. Sleep and that kind of stillness are gifts that God particularly wants to give us, because without them it is almost impossible to receive the greatest gift, the quiet presence of God.

The trouble with talking about asceticism is that it sounds weird; the life of prayer by this description might sound a little precious, not quite normal. I think the psalm itself answers that objection with its dominant image. The prayerful person is

> . . . like a tree
> planted by water channels,
> which gives its fruit in its season,
> and its leaf does not wither;
> and everything she does will prosper.
> *(v. 3)*

So what do you think—would you call a tree like that "normal"? It is not ordinary, at least not in the semiarid land of Israel, where a tree like that is a sign of life to anyone on a journey. A tree like that stands out on the horizon and tells a traveler, "There's water here." Its spreading branches offer rest in the shade, protection and respite from the burning heat. A Christian whose life is shaped by deep prayer should be like that tree: not ostentatious, yet hardly unnoticeable. People who are on a journey and in need will notice—people looking for shelter from the heat, people who are desperate for water. Who knows? Some few people might be attracted just because a full-grown life of prayer is a beautiful thing to see.

There is a short Jewish prayer that is said when someone catches sight of a particularly beautiful tree:

בָּרוּךְ אַתָּה יְיָ אֱלֹהֵינוּ מֶלֶךְ הָעוֹלָם שֶׁכָּכָה לוֹ בְּעוֹלָמוֹ:
(*barûkh ʾattah YHWH ʾelohênû melekh haʿôlam shekakhah lô beʿôlamô*)
Blessed are you, O Lord, King of the Universe, who has something like this in his world.

Now imagine: what if our own dedicated lives of prayer and meditation on God's Word would merit that same compliment for God—"Blessed are you, O Lord, King of the Universe, who has something like this in his world"? May it be so for each of us. Amen.

THE TEXT IN PREACHING CONTEXT

Two aspects of context are important for the development of this sermon: literary and liturgical context. With respect to the former, my assumption is that the Psalter is a carefully edited book. (This is generally a safe assumption for all the books of the Bible.) No careful editor is going to be casual about the beginning of a book. Since the Psalter is a book of prayers, the first psalm, though not itself a prayer, is seeking to establish a disposition that will enable us to make good use of all the prayers that follow. With respect to liturgical context, the Revised Common Lectionary (Year C) appoints this psalm for use on the penultimate Sunday of the Epiphany season, ten days before Ash Wednesday.[12] Again, I assume that this reflects deliberate choice, signaling that this is an appropriate time for the church to hear the psalm's teaching about the kind of life that has substance in God's eyes:

> For YHWH knows the way of the righteous,
> but the way of the wicked vanishes.
>
> *(v. 6)*

Because the psalms are poems, matters of word choice and translation are especially important, and so I began by pointing out that the very first word carries connotations of privilege. From the perspective of the Israelite wisdom tradition (to which this psalm belongs), discipline is more like a gift than (as we too often see it) a punishment—even though it may be a difficult gift to receive.[13] The discipline that comes from God is a token of esteem:

> Privileged is the person whom you discipline, YHWH,
> and from your Teaching (*torah*) you instruct him.
>
> *(Ps. 94:12)*

Therefore, in suggesting that my hearers exercise discipline with respect to television, I deliberately did *not* tell them, "It will give you more time to study," since most of my students already feel overworked, and not wholly without cause. I offered them rest rather than more work, and when I said that, there was an audible sigh of longing in the chapel.

That suggestion of watching less television in order to have more rest is countercultural, as most biblical preaching must be. Therefore, I had to answer the obvious objection—in this case, of elitism. Exploring the psalmist's image of the tree provided the answer to that objection. That is, I did not have to mount a persuasively reasoned argument for an unpopular cause (which would probably have been unconvincing in the end). I only had to make the image present in the text vivid to their minds, and let it do the work of persuasion.

---

12. In York Chapel at Duke Divinity School, the readings for the Wednesday Eucharist are those appointed for the previous Sunday. This sermon was then preached exactly a week before Ash Wednesday.

13. In the biblical wisdom literature, "discipline" is invariably a positive concept (e.g., Prov. 12:1; 15:32). For further development of this idea, see Ellen F. Davis, *Proverbs, Ecclesiastes, and the Song of Songs* (Louisville, Ky.: Westminster John Knox, 2000), 25–26, 99–100, etc.

Psalm 22

Christ Church, Alexandria, Virginia
Good Friday 1998

Blessed is the wood by which righteousness comes.
Wis. 14:7 NRSV

This is the day when language turns back on itself, when we cannot speak without contradicting ourselves, on this sour-sweet day of death that we call Good. The cross stands over all our words and thoughts this day as the sign and source of contradiction: the instrument of shameful death by whose virtue, as our anthem says—by whose *virtue* joy has come to the whole world.[14] Centuries ago, Christians gave poetic expression to the contradiction of the cross with the legend that Calvary was the very place where once the garden of Eden had been, that the deadly cross rose up there as another Tree of Life, watered by the blood of the second and perfect Adam.

> My God, my God, why have you forsaken me?
>   Why are you so far from helping me, from the words of my
>   groaning?
> *(Ps. 22:1 NRSV [2 Heb.])*[15]

It is no coincidence that Jesus' cry from the cross of contradiction echoes the opening verse of the most contradictory of all the psalms. Psalm 22 reads almost like two different and opposite psalms pasted together, a prayer of anguish joined with an exultant hymn of praise. Seeing how those two opposites are joined together will help us better understand this sour-sweet day, this Good day of death.

Psalm 22 begins with those horrible cries of pain and accusation directed against God:

14. Anthem 1, *BCP*, 281.
15. Scripture quotations in this sermon, except where otherwise noted, are from the NRSV.

152

> O my God, I cry by day, but you do not answer;
> and by night, but [I] find no rest.
> . . . .
> Many bulls encircle me,
> . . . .
> they open wide their mouths at me,
> like a ravening and roaring lion.
> . . . .
> My heart is like wax;
> it is melted within my breast.
> *(vv. 2, 12–14 [3, 13–15 Heb.])*

Thus the psalmist plummets, like Job, deeper and deeper into his agony, further and further, it seems, away from God, until he reaches bottom and hurls that stunning accusation at God: "You lay me in the dust of death" (v. 15 [16 Heb.]). "You [God] lay me in the dust of death."

Then suddenly, with no apparent logic, the psalmist appeals for help to the God whom he has just declared to be the enemy. At first he speaks cautiously, asking only not to be completely abandoned: "But you, O Lord, do not be far away!" (v. 19 [20 Heb.]). Then he grows more insistent; God must act—now. "Deliver me from the sword . . . from the power of the dog, save me from the lion's mouth, from the horns of wild oxen—you have answered me!" (vv. 20–21 AT [21–22 Heb.]). The recognition is that sudden and that surprising—so surprising that a lot of translators through the centuries have changed the text of verse 21 (22 Heb.) because they could not believe what the Hebrew so plainly says. In the middle of a sentence, mouth open for one more tortured scream for deliverance, the psalmist in a flash knows that the battle is over, the victory won: "From the horns of wild oxen—you have answered me!" The translation we're using today reads "you have rescued me," but that is more than the Hebrew says, and more also than we witness this day—for surely Jesus was not "rescued" from the cross, in any ordinary sense of that word. The psalmist may still be pinned on the horns of wild oxen, yet suddenly he knows beyond doubting that God has answered, and that changes everything. God's answer changes cries of abandonment and outrage, desperate pleas, to praise, wave upon wave of praise. And now the anguished psalmist, the one who was as good as dead, thrust into the grave by God's own hand, now he is calling all Israel to sing the Hallelujah Chorus to the God who answers prayer:

> For he did not despise or abhor
>   the affliction of the afflicted;
> he did not hide his face from me,
>   but heard when I cried to him.
>   *(v. 24 [25 Heb.])*

This contradictory psalm ends with praise as extravagant as the accusations were fierce. The psalmist's praise eddies out in circles expanding endlessly through time and space: the psalmist's friends and family, the people Israel, all the nations of the world, even the dead shall rise up from their graves and start belting out psalms to "proclaim [God's] deliverance to a people yet unborn, saying that [God] has done it" (v. 31 [32 Heb.])—saying that God has done it, done it all.

But note: that praise is not an apology; the psalmist never takes back the accusation against God. Yet he praises the God who delivers him, knowing well it is the same God whose hand laid him in the dust of death. The psalmist offers his anguish and his fury along with his joy as a single witness to the strange, saving work that God has done. The accusation and the praise stand together, a contradictory witness. And it is just because it is contradictory that we know this to be a true witness to a mystery, to the strangest and darkest part of our life with God: the mystery of faithful suffering.

We prefer to think of suffering as a problem, not a mystery. Problems have explanations and solutions, and so, like Job's friends, we offer ours, hopeful that if we are clever enough, we can get on top of this problem of suffering. But the idea that suffering is nothing more than a problem to be solved is a religious delusion, a heresy, and like all heresies, it deprives those who believe it of a true relationship with God. The psalmist shows us the truth: suffering is a part of our life with God that no one escapes, not even God's only begotten Son. Suffering is a fearful mystery that beckons us to go deeper in prayer, in anguished and angry prayer, deeper into our pain, until we are drawn finally into the heart of God.

The psalmist shows us the moment of astonished discovery to which faithful suffering leads: the moment when, cast down into the depths, cast down even by God's hand, there we discover, beyond all logic and imagining, that the bottom of despair is solid. And suddenly we know, with strange but unshakable certainty, that we cannot fall—in life or in death, we cannot fall beyond the reach of God's love and power to save. It is out of that certainty that we discover our own boundless capacity for praise.

The cry from the cross—"My God, my God, why have you forsaken me?"—Jesus' cry points to the whole movement that the psalmist traces for us: from anguish to joy, joy that bursts out in the midst of suffering, the joy of a heart that does not shun suffering but plummets to the bottom of it and finds that the bottom of my despair lies within the heart of God. Joy like that is not a mood to which we can work ourselves up; it is a gift from God, the one thing that we most need and cannot coerce, the gift of joy that triumphs over suffering. It is a gift we must prepare ourselves carefully to receive. Christians have traditionally understood the season of Lent as a time devoted particularly to that work of preparation, when we practice more deliberately than usual the difficult but certain movement toward God called "walking in the way of the cross."

Walking in the way of the cross—what does that really look like on the ground? It is not, of course, an activity confined to this one season or week or day of the year; it is the basic movement of the whole Christian life. But what does that mean in concrete terms, on an ordinary day in the life of any one of us? Simply this: walking in the way of the cross is opening yourself to the pain that comes to you, in whatever measure it comes—not looking for pain, not accepting it without question or protest, but rather living with pain honestly and generously, living in a way that gives hope to others.

The way of the cross traces a different route in each of our lives. For one, that way leads through chronic depression; for another, physical incapacity. In one life, the trauma of premature death; in another, the quieter sorrows of old age. The way of the cross takes us through loneliness and troubled relationships, the loss of those we love most. It leads through betrayal, keenly felt disappointments, and confrontation with our own deep shame. Walking that way with our eyes open takes courage, for it requires that we see the world as it really is: a place of profound suffering, where God's love pursues us into the depths, enfolds us, sustains us, and finally brings us up to joy. Continuing on that way teaches us spiritual economy, so that gradually we shed the heavy pretense of self-sufficiency, lightening our load until we become, like the psalmist, quick to confess our desperate need, eager to discover and celebrate the strange grace that God is working in our lives.

And that is how we will know that we are beginning to get the hang of it, this walking in the way of the cross. We will know when we begin to feel lighter, lighter even though we take with full seriousness the pain we feel and see around us. We will know because that extraordinary lightness in the midst of pain is the mark of our Crucified Savior, the

One who was so free of himself that on the cross he could yield himself fully to God: "Into your hands I commend my spirit" (Luke 23:46). Jesus' cross is finally not the place of abandonment but the place where he who has made himself so light is taken up fully into the strange saving work of God.

The sixteenth-century martyr and mystical poet St. John of the Cross made a pen-and-ink drawing that expresses in a striking way the lightness of the Crucified One. St. John received this image of our Crucified Lord in a vision. The perspective is vertical, looking down on the cross;

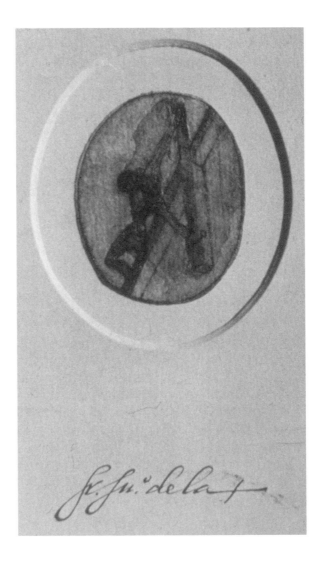

it's a God's-eye view of the crucifixion. Jesus' delicate frame appears in marked contrast with the heavy wood beams. There is a kind of propulsion movement, so that Jesus' whole upper body is thrust forward, with only his hands held to the crossbeam by the large nails. The legs are light but powerful: knees bent, calf muscles taut, hips and feet pressed flat against the vertical beam; it's as though he's poised to push off. The man on the cross is a bird straining to leave the tree behind; the hard wood is the branch that gives him purchase for flight. The same cross that punishes his body steadies him to soar into the heart of God. This is indeed a visionary's drawing, for in only a few square inches John has captured the full dimensions of that vast movement of Christ's passion: the movement through the depths of suffering that brings us home to God. It is an image to anchor our hope this day, this sour-sweet day of death that we call Good, when "walking in the way of the cross, [we] find it none other than the way of life and peace."[16] Amen.

THE TEXT IN PREACHING CONTEXT

Good Friday is theologically the most challenging day of the Christian year, as its paradoxical name suggests. The anthem cited at the beginning of the sermon points to the mystery that lies at the heart of the Christian faith, and this day in particular:

> We glory in your cross, O Lord,
> and praise and glorify your holy resurrection;
> for by virtue of your cross
> joy has come to the whole world.

The Good Friday liturgy is also (at least, in many Episcopal churches, such as the one where this was preached) the most lengthy and complex liturgy of the year. In contrast to the complexity of the occasion, the sermon design is extremely simple. I followed the structure of the psalm, focusing on the moment when it suddenly turns, mid-verse, from lament into praise. Psalm 22 is unique in that it conjoins one of the most strident laments in the Psalter with the most extended "vow of praise." In the latter, a standard component in lament psalms, the one who cries out

---

16. The quotation is from the Collect for Monday in Holy Week:

Almighty God, whose most dear Son went not up to joy but first he suffered pain, and entered not into glory before he was crucified: Mercifully grant that we, walking in the way of the cross, may find it none other than the way of life and peace; through Jesus Christ your Son our Lord, who lives and reigns with you and the Holy Spirit, one God, for ever and ever. *Amen.* (*BCP*, 220)

for deliverance typically promises to share with others the good news of God's saving action. What is remarkable here is not only the length but the scope of that promise of praise. While the psalmists usually hold out no hope of life after death (e.g., Ps. 6), here the dead are specifically included among those who will offer praise for what God has done.[17]

Psalm 22 is of course central to the Passion Narrative in the Gospels, but the extravagance of both lamentation and praise, as well as their shocking conjunction, make the psalm itself an important text for probing the mystery of Good Friday.

17. Cf. Ellen F. Davis, "Exploding the Limits: Form and Function in Psalm 22," *Journal for the Study of the Old Testament* 53 (1992): 93–105; reprinted in *The Poetical Books: A Sheffield Reader*, ed. David J. A. Clines (Sheffield: Sheffield Academic Press, 1997), 135–46.

Scripture Index

References are listed according to the standard English numbering. Bracketed references are to the Hebrew text.